Refurbishment and Upgrading of Buildings

Refurbishment and Upgrading of Buildings

David Highfield

London and New York

To Christine

First published 2000
by E & FN Spon
11 New Fetter Lane, London EC4P 4EE

Simultaneously published in the USA and Canada
by E & FN Spon
29 West 35th Street, New York, NY 10001

E & FN Spon is an imprint of the Taylor & Francis Group

Typeset in Gill by
Keystroke, Jacaranda Lodge, Wolverhampton
Printed and bound in Great Britain by
St Edmundsbury Press, Bury St Edmunds, Suffolk

British Library Cataloguing in Publication Data
A catalogue record for this book is available from the British
Library

Library of Congress Cataloging in Publication Data
Highfield, David.
    Refurbishment and upgrading of buildings / David Highfield.
        p.   cm.
    Includes bibliographical references and index.
    1. Buildings—Repair and reconstruction.   I. Title.
TH3401 .H53 2000
690'.24—dc21   99–057572/0

ISBN 0–419–23160–9

Contents

Introduction

Building refurbishment and upgrading (including maintenance, repair, restoration and extension) – all broadly categorised as 'repair and maintenance' by the Government for statistical purposes – is a major component of construction activity, having consistently accounted for just under half of the construction industry's total output for most of the 1990s. The Government Department of the Environment, Transport and the Regions categorises construction output into 'new work' and 'repair and maintenance', and between 1994 and the first quarter of 1999 the value of repair and maintenance work has averaged, annually, some 49% of the total of all work carried out by the construction industry (DETR 1999: *Information Bulletin 599).*

Building owners and developers have, in recent years, come to realise the potential value of our vast stock of old, redundant and obsolete buildings as a means of providing, through their refurbishment and re-use, high-quality 'modern' accommodation more quickly, and at a lower cost, than the alternative of new construction. Refurbishment can provide 'new' accommodation in only half to three-quarters of the time needed for the alternative of demolition and new construction, and at only 50–80% of the cost, resulting in considerable financial benefits to the developer.

There has also been a significant change in attitudes favouring the conservation and recycling of resources during the past 25 years. The wholesale demolition and redevelopment policies of the 1960s and 1970s resulted in the replacement of large numbers of basically sound buildings, often with buildings of much poorer quality, particularly in the housing sector. It is now widely recognised that it makes far greater sense to retain and refurbish buildings in preference to demolishing and replacing them.

The latter years of the twentieth century have also seen an increasing worldwide focus on sustainability and the protection of our environment. It has been recognised that the recycling of materials and products is, in the majority of cases, more environmentally friendly than simply disposing of them when they reach the end of, what is perceived to be, their useful life. There is no better example of the environmental benefits of effective sustainability in practice than the recycling of buildings. For every building that is recycled through refurbishment, the extraction of raw materials and the manufacturing processes and energy involved in converting these into a completed replacement building are avoided to the undoubted benefit of the environment.

Current Government environmental policy on housing is also encouraging the refurbishment and re-use of buildings by prescribing that 60% of the 4.4 million new homes needed by 2016 should be provided on previously developed brownfield sites in order to reduce the loss of countryside. As many of these brownfield sites – the majority of which are within towns and cities – already have redundant or obsolete buildings standing on them, an increase in refurbishment activity will inevitably result. A further means by which the Government has sought to increase building refurbishment is the exemption from Value Added Tax (VAT) for schemes involving the conversion of commercial premises to housing, one result of which has been a significant increase in the refurbishment of city-centre office buildings to provide 'new' homes.

The Urban Task Force, set up by the Government to establish a new vision for urban regeneration, made recommendations, which, if implemented, will further encourage building refurbishment: one of the key measures proposed by the Task Force is the implementation of a strategy for the recycling of land and buildings which includes making the best use of derelict, vacant and underused land and buildings before carrying out new development on greenfield sites. The Urban Task Force also recommended the harmonisation of taxation laws on newbuild and residential conversions, which, at the time, discriminated against refurbishment by imposing VAT at a punitive rate of 17.5% on the renovation of empty dwellings, whilst new housebuilding was exempt (DETR 1999: *Final Report*).

All of the aforementioned factors, together with the many other advantages to be gained, will ensure that the refurbishment and re-use of buildings will continue to represent a major, and increasing, component of construction activity well into the twenty-first century and beyond. It is therefore essential that all of those associated with building refurbishment and re-use remain fully conversant with the key issues involved and, in particular, the complex technological aspects peculiar to this type of work. In addressing a wide range of technological problems, and the solutions used to resolve them, this book should prove to be an invaluable aid to building owners, developers, architects, surveyors, and main and specialist contractors involved with the refurbishment, maintenance, repair, restoration and upgrading of buildings. It should also be of value to students of architecture, building and construction management, and surveying in their study of this increasingly important area.

The first section poses the question 'Why refurbishment?', and explains the reasons for, and advantages to be gained from, opting to refurbish and re-use existing buildings, rather than demolishing and replacing them with new buildings. This should enable building owners and developers to undertake a more comprehensive analysis when appraising potential refurbishment schemes.

Section 2 examines the problems of ensuring that elements within existing buildings have the appropriate fire-resistance. The section first outlines the key statutory requirements and goes on to give detailed explanations of the techniques that can be used to upgrade the fire-resistance of existing elements so that they comply with relevant regulations.

Section 3 deals with upgrading of the internal surfaces of walls and floors, explaining the methods used to restore surface finishes that have deteriorated beyond repair, and the provision of new finishes in buildings

where none originally existed, for example in agricultural barns and older factories.

Section 4 looks at upgrading the thermal performance of existing walls and roofs to meet the statutory requirements relating to energy conservation; and as a means of improving comfort, and reducing the 'running costs' of buildings. A wide range of internally and externally applied thermal upgrading methods are explained in detail, together with the actual reductions in heat loss that are possible.

Section 5 addresses the problem of upgrading the acoustic performance of existing walls and floors, and the techniques that can be employed to improve their sound-insulating capabilities to comply with legislation aimed at preventing noise nuisance between different occupancies.

Section 6 deals with the prevention of intrusive moisture and dampness within buildings, including damp penetration through walls, ground floors and roofs. The section also explains the causes and effects of condensation, and the ways in which it can be eliminated.

Section 7 examines the causes and main forms of timber decay, including fungal and insect attack, the treatments that can be used to eradicate them, and the techniques available for preventing further attacks. A wide range of methods used for the physical repair and reinstatement of decayed structural timber elements, including beams, joists and roof members, is explained.

In some refurbishment schemes it is necessary to strengthen existing timber floors so that they can support greater applied loadings, and Section 8 describes, and gives a comparative evaluation of, the techniques used to achieve this.

Section 9 looks at heavy-lifting technology, which is gradually becoming more common in the refurbishment of buildings. A brief account of its capabilities in moving whole buildings is given, followed by a detailed description of its use in raising the height of a complete roof structure.

The underpinning of existing foundations is often found to be necessary in refurbishment and alteration work, especially where older buildings are involved, or where a change of use will impose greater loads on the substructure. Section 10 explains the principal reasons for underpinning, and describes a wide range of techniques used, from traditional to more complex systems.

Section 11 deals with facade retention, an extreme, and often controversial, form of building re-use. The key technical problems associated with erecting an entirely new structure behind a retained facade are described, along with the solutions used to solve them.

Throughout the text, numerous references are made to specific proprietary systems and products and, for those wishing to obtain further information on these, the details of their manufacturers are given in Section 12.

A key feature of this book is the large number of detailed line drawings which support the text and enhance the reader's understanding of the techniques used in the refurbishment and upgrading of buildings. Thanks are due to Adrian Riley of Leeds Metropolitan University for his painstaking work in preparing these for final publication.

References

Department of Environment, Transport and the Regions (1999) *Final Report of the Urban Taskforce*, DETR, London.

Department of Environment, Transport and the Regions (1999) *Information Bulletin 599: Output and Employment in the Construction Industry*, DETR, London.

Wood, R. (1998) 'Value Added Tax: Implications for Historic Buildings', *The Building Conservation Directory 1998*, ed. J. Taylor, Cathedral Communications Ltd, Tisbury, 46–7.

1
Why refurbishment?

1.1 General

The provision of modern accommodation through the refurbishment and upgrading of existing old, redundant or obsolete buildings, in preference to constructing new buildings, has increased considerably in recent years, and there are many reasons for this. Most of the reasons can be attributed to the specific advantages that can be gained by opting for refurbishment rather than newbuild, although in some cases there may be legislative constraints, such as those concerned with listed buildings, which leave developers with no choice but to retain and refurbish certain buildings.

Where a developer wishes to provide modern accommodation, and a suitable existing building is available in the right location, all of the following points should be carefully considered since it is likely that refurbishment and re-use of the building may well be a more viable means of providing the accommodation than opting for new construction.

1.2 The availability of buildings suitable for refurbishment

Advances in industry and commerce, together with society's constant demand for improved interior environments for both work and leisure, have led to large numbers of buildings becoming outdated, redundant or obsolete and this, in turn, has provided an abundant supply of buildings suitable for refurbishment and conversion to new uses. Examples include large numbers of old factory and warehouse buildings in industrial centres, and outdated institutional buildings such as

schools and hospitals – the latter as a result of Government policies in the late 1980s and 1990s which led to the closure of large numbers of asylums throughout the country. Changes in transportation systems during the nineteenth and twentieth centuries from river and canal transport to railways and, finally, to the motorway network have led to large numbers of riverside and canalside factories and warehouses and railway buildings becoming redundant as industry and commerce have had to relocate to be near the new transportation arteries. This has led to a considerable amount of refurbishment and re-use of redundant riverside, canalside and dockside buildings in recent years as developers have come to realise the value and desirability of waterside locations for housing, offices and bars and restaurants. As recently introduced planning policies have become more favourable to housing development in cities there has been an increase in the refurbishment and conversion of city-centre office buildings into flats to enable people to live close to their work and reduce demands on transportation systems. Another major source of buildings suitable for refurbishment and re-use are the many churches that have become redundant since the 1970s. Changing population patterns, and the declining position of the church in people's lives, have resulted in thousands of churches becoming available for redevelopment; from large city churches to small village chapels that have been successfully refurbished and converted into residential, office, recreational and manufacturing accommodation. In addition to the above examples, the existing housing stock represents a major focus for refurbishment activity. The Government estimated, from information derived from the 1996 English House Condition Survey, that in England there is a £10 billion backlog of renovation needed in the local authority housing stock alone (Housing and Regeneration Policy: A Statement by the Deputy Prime Minister, John Prescott, 22 July 1998).

In the absence of open sites available for new development, particularly in the prime commercial and residential areas of most of our towns and cities, developers seeking to provide modern accommodation have no choice but to focus on existing buildings. Having located a suitable building, the developer must then decide whether to demolish it and construct a new building or to opt for a refurbishment scheme, and the remaining sections explain why the latter course is often chosen.

1.3 The quality of buildings suitable for refurbishment

A further major factor in favour of the refurbishment of old, redundant or obsolete buildings, in addition to their widespread availability, is that many of these buildings are well built and structurally sound. Many may be run-down, neglected and unfit for modern usage as they stand, but the tried and tested methods of construction used to build them have left potential developers with an abundant legacy of sound, durable structures which provide an ideal basis for refurbishment and re-use. However, it should not be assumed that such buildings are always of high structural quality, and it is essential that any building being considered for refurbishment, even though it may appear to be sound, is subjected to a detailed survey in order to confirm its quality and condition, and to ascertain the likely cost of any repairs deemed necessary and their effect on the feasibility of going ahead with a refurbishment scheme.

1.4 The shorter development period

One of the principal advantages of opting for refurbishment and re-use of an existing building – rather than demolition and new construction – is that, in the majority of cases, the 'new' accommodation will be available in a much shorter time.

The work required to refurbish an existing building will normally take considerably less time than the alternative of demolition, site clearance and the construction of a new building, unless the refurbishment involves, for example, extensive structural alterations or remodelling. In addition to the time saved during the building works phase, time is also saved during the pre-contract design and planning permission phases, which normally take much longer for new development than for refurbishment, even where a change of use is proposed for the existing building. These time savings, during the pre-contract design, planning permission and building works phases of development often mean that opting for refurbishment can provide the new accommodation in only half to three-quarters of the time needed for demolition and new construction, giving the following financial benefits:

- The shorter contract duration reduces the effects of inflation on building costs.
- The shorter overall development period reduces the cost of financing the scheme.
- The client obtains the building sooner, and therefore begins to earn revenue from it (for example, rentals, retail sales or manufacturing profits) at an earlier date.

1.5 The economic advantages

The cost of refurbishing and re-using an existing building is generally considerably less than the cost of demolition and new construction, since many of the building elements are already constructed. However, the existing construction and its condition will have a considerable bearing on the costs of refurbishment. For example, if the existing floor-to-ceiling heights are either too low or too high for the proposed new use, the necessary adjustments may be very costly, as illustrated by the Granary Building scheme in Leeds (see Section 9.3) where the entire roof structure had to be raised by 300mm in order to allow re-use of the uppermost storey. Also, many older industrial buildings have exposed timber floors, supported by timber or cast-iron columns and beams which require upgrading to comply with current fire-protection legislation (see Section 2). In addition, new fire-escape stairs and enclosures will almost certainly be required, all of which will add to the costs of the refurbishment scheme. If the building is in a poor physical condition because of neglect, deterioration or vandalism, the refurbishment will also involve the expense of repair and restoration work which may have a significant effect on overall costs.

Against costs of this nature, the developer must weigh the potential savings achieved by re-using most of the existing elements of the building, and the shorter development period with its associated financial benefits outlined in Section 1.4 above.

There would be little point in refurbishing and re-using existing buildings if the costs were to be greater than those of demolition and new construction, unless overriding reasons exist, as in the case of buildings which have been listed because of their architectural or historic interest. Refurbishment and re-use will be substantially cheaper than demolition and new construction only where a suitable building is selected which is in a reasonable physical condition, and which does not require excessive structural alterations in order to adapt it to its proposed new use.

In the majority of cases, the decision regarding whether or not to refurbish and re-use an existing building will revolve around the potential economic advantages. It is essential, therefore, that – in the first instance – a detailed cost-appraisal of alternative refurbishment schemes versus demolition and newbuild is carried out, since this, above all else, will normally determine whether or not refurbishment is viable.

The most important factors that determine whether or not refurbishment is viable are:

- the expected rental income (in developments for letting)
- the expected capital value (in developments to be sold after completion)
- the estimated cost of development
- the cost of acquiring the site
- the cost of financing the scheme.

1.5.1 Expected rental income

The expected rental income from a refurbished building will depend on several factors:

- the proposed new use(s) for the building
- the location of the building
- the relative attractiveness of the area in which the building stands, including the amenity of the surrounding area and its accessibility

- the quality of the accommodation and services after refurbishment which, in turn, will depend upon the standard of refurbishment carried out
- the level of demand for such accommodation from new firms setting up or moving into the area, and existing firms wishing to expand or improve their accommodation
- the availability of other, similar accommodation in the area.

Details of prevailing rentals, and the extent of demand for different types of accommodation in an area, are best obtained from local property/letting agents.

1.5.2 Expected capital value

The expected capital value on completion of the refurbishment scheme will depend upon those factors, listed above, which affect expected rental income.

1.5.3 Estimated cost of development

The development cost for a refurbishment scheme will depend on several factors, the most important of which are as follows:

1.5.3.1 The proposed new use

The proposed new use for the refurbished building can have a significant effect upon the development costs. For example, the cost of refurbishing a late nineteenth-century warehouse to provide utilitarian manufacturing accommodation would be considerably less than converting it to high-specification, prestige office accommodation.

1.5.3.2 The standard of refurbishment envisaged

The required standard or quality of the proposed accommodation will have a significant effect on the final cost of refurbishment. For example, the existing windows may be in sufficiently good condition to warrant only minor repair and repainting, but the developer may wish to replace them with new metal or uPVC windows with sealed double glazing in order to improve their appearance and thermal properties and to reduce maintenance.

Opting for the latter will clearly significantly increase the cost of refurbishment.

Decisions regarding building services can also significantly affect the final cost of a refurbishment scheme. For example, where a building is being refurbished to provide modern office accommodation, the choice of a simple hot-water radiator heating system, with openable windows to provide natural ventilation, will cost considerably less than a sophisticated mechanical heating, ventilation and air-conditioning system. Costs can also be reduced in taller buildings by installing fewer passenger lifts, or even no lifts at all in buildings of only two or three storeys.

Virtually every design decision relating to the quality, standard or amenity of the refurbished building will have a direct effect on the final cost of the scheme – the higher the specification, the higher the overall cost of the completed building. However, as stated in 1.5.1 above, in the long term, the greater costs incurred by providing a higher standard of refurbishment can be recouped by the higher rental income (or resale value) that such standards can demand.

1.5.3.3 The age of the building

Generally, the older the building and the longer it has been empty, the greater will be the costs of repairing and restoring the existing structure and fabric. In many cases, where the building has remained empty and neglected for a prolonged period, dampness, which is the principal agent in most forms of building deterioration, may well have penetrated, leading to timber decay and damage to finishes. Empty, neglected buildings often fall victim to vandalism, the results of which may be very expensive to rectify. These factors apart, the basic fact that a building is old will mean that certain items will need attention because of their natural deterioration over a long period of time. In addition, items that may still be in good condition will often need replacing merely because they are obsolete or outdated in their design, common examples being sanitary fixtures and fittings and lift installations.

In many refurbishment schemes it will be found that overall costs are directly proportional to the age of the building and the degree of neglect it has suffered, and the proposed refurbishment of any old, neglected building should therefore be given very careful consideration before proceeding. For this reason, it is vital that the first stage of any feasibility study should comprise a detailed survey of the building in order to establish the precise extent and costs of any works required to repair and restore the structure and fabric to a reasonable standard.

1.5.3.4 The construction of the building

The construction of the existing building can have a significant effect on the cost of refurbishment; fire protection often being a key factor, particularly where older buildings are concerned. Many older buildings have timber stairs and floors which may be supported by unprotected cast-iron or steel beams and columns, and these will have to be upgraded or replaced to comply with current fire regulations. The upgrading, or replacement, of existing timber and cast-iron or steel elements to comply with current fire regulations, including means of escape, often proves to be one of the most costly areas of building refurbishment. Section 2 explains the current statutory requirements with regard to fire-resistance and explains the techniques used to upgrade the fire-resistance of existing elements of construction.

Another common example of potentially high costs in building refurbishment is the strengthening or replacement of existing floor structures where their load-carrying capacities are inadequate to meet the requirements of the proposed new use. In such cases it will be necessary either to carry out strengthening operations or to replace the existing floors completely with new floors, usually of in-situ or precast concrete. Section 8 describes the techniques that can be used to strengthen existing timber floor structures.

1.5.4 The cost of acquiring the site

The cost of acquiring the freehold or leasehold of the site should never exceed the difference between the capital value of the completed development and the development costs, since, if it does, a financial loss will be incurred. It is therefore very important to assess accurately the proper value of the site which will largely be determined by the following factors:

- the location of the site, which will decide the potential users of the refurbished building

- the uses for which planning permission can be obtained
- the expected rental income from, or capital value of, the refurbished building
- the total development costs.

1.5.5 The cost of financing the refurbishment scheme

The cost of financing the scheme will depend principally on the following factors:

- the cost of the refurbishment works
- the duration of the scheme
- the level of interest rates prevailing at the time of the scheme.

In the majority of cases the total interest payable on money borrowed to finance a refurbishment scheme will be significantly less than that for new construction, owing to the lower overall costs and shorter development periods generally associated with refurbishment schemes. In addition, when interest rates are higher, the refurbishment option will become even more attractive, since this will result in a greater differential between the costs of financing refurbishment and the higher costs of financing new construction schemes.

Detailed consideration of the factors discussed above will be essential if the correct decision is to be made on the type and level of refurbishment or, indeed, whether the refurbishment option is viable at all. Of equal importance to examining all of the salient factors is ensuring that designers, building surveyors and building economists with a high level of expertise in refurbishment work are commissioned to prepare alternative schemes, carry out surveys and complete cost-feasibility studies. Construction firms specialising in refurbishment work should also be consulted at the feasibility stage to advise the design team on aspects such as buildability. Only if this is done can the developer be sure of opting for the scheme that will give the best value for money, whilst remaining within a realistic budget.

1.6 The availability of financial aid

In the majority of cases, the refurbishment option is chosen for economic reasons – because it costs the developer less than newbuild, and a further major incentive, therefore (and one which can make the refurbishment option even more attractive), is the availability of various forms of financial aid. Financial aid, in the form of grants and 'soft' loans, is not available for all refurbishment schemes, but in many cases – for example where sub-standard housing or historic buildings are concerned, where jobs are being created, or urban regeneration is taking place – it may be possible to obtain substantial grants towards the cost of the work. Financial aid for the refurbishment, repair, conservation, restoration and maintenance of buildings is available from a large number of different bodies and it is beyond the scope of this book to identify them all. Some examples of grant-awarding sources include English Heritage, which makes grants towards the costs of repair, conservation and restoration of historic (usually listed) buildings; local authorities, which administer housing improvement grant schemes; and the Government Department of the Environment, Transport and the Regions Single Regeneration Budget, which provides funding for a wide range of projects focusing on sustainable development, including bringing redundant buildings back into use and housing refurbishment.

Sources of finance range from public funds, provided by central government and local authorities, to private funds from banks, insurance companies, building societies, and so on.

The main categories of financial aid are:

- Loans
  A loan is a sum of money lent to the recipient which must be repaid to the lender over an agreed period, at an agreed rate of interest. The rate of interest charged for a normal loan will be at the current commercial rate.

- Soft loans
  A soft loan is similar in principle to a normal loan, with the important exception that the rate of interest charged will be *below* the current commercial rate.

- Grants
  A grant is a sum of money awarded towards the cost of a scheme which the recipient is not required to repay.

Many sources of financial aid are subjected to specific conditions and restrictions with which the recipient must comply. These vary considerably, and details should be obtained from the various awarding bodies. However, the following points apply to many of the loans and grants that are available:

- The award of a loan or grant will normally only be made if the scheme is viable.
- Awards are often restricted to schemes that would be unable to proceed without the receipt of financial aid.
- Awards for a specific aspect of the work may not be duplicated where more than one source of funding is available.
- Awards are normally made on completion of the work, unless it is a large scheme, in which case the award may be made in instalments.
- Generally, awards must be applied for, and approved, before the scheme commences, although it will normally also be necessary to have obtained planning permission.
- The majority of awards are discretionary.
- Loans and grants normally provide only a part of the total funding necessary for refurbishment schemes, and only rarely are awards of 100% made. Thus, for the majority of schemes, the loan or grant will represent a maximum of half the total cost of the scheme, and often it is less than this.
- The funds available for financial aid are strictly limited in the majority of cases, with demand exceeding supply.

Generally, awards are made on a 'first come, first served' basis or by the use of specific priority criteria.

It is clear, therefore, that if the refurbishment option being considered for an existing building is eligible for grant, or even soft loan, aid, and a grant or loan can be obtained, the refurbishment option will become even more attractive when compared with the alternative of demolition and new construction.

1.7 Planning permission may not be required

Under section 57 of the Town and Country Planning Act 1990, planning permission is required for 'development'. However, section 55 (2) (a) of the Act states that 'the carrying out of works for the maintenance, improvement or other alteration of any building *which affect only the interior of the building, or do not materially affect the external appearance of the building*' [my italics] does not constitute development. Such works, therefore, do *not* require planning permission. Thus, if the refurbishment scheme does not affect the exterior appearance of the building, there may be no need for the developer to obtain planning permission, resulting in a further shortening of the development period, and a corresponding saving in costs.

However, it should be noted that a key exception to the above, as detailed in section 55 (2) (f) of the Act, is where the 'use class' of the building changes, in which case planning permission will still be required. The Town and Country Planning (Use Classes) Order 1987 (as amended in 1991) designates sixteen use classes, and any proposed change from one of these use classes to another will require planning permission even if the external appearance of the building does not change. An example of this might be where it is proposed to refurbish and convert a riverside warehouse (use class B8, 'Storage or distribution') into a hotel (use class C1, 'Hotels and hostels'). There are, though, numerous examples of refurbishment schemes which do not require planning permission, some of the most common examples being the interior upgrading and alteration of old, outdated office buildings to provide modern office accommodation and the refurbishment and modernisation of unfit housing: the refurbished building remains in the same use class and it is therefore permissible to carry out extensive interior alterations without the need for planning permission. The extent of the works might go as far as completely gutting the building and providing an entirely new internal structure, as in facade retention (see Section 11), provided the exterior appearance remains the same.

1.8 The effects of plot ratio control

Plot ratio control, which was introduced by the Ministry of Town and Country Planning in 1948, is a device used by planning authorities to restrict the amount of floor space provided in new buildings in relation to their site areas. For example, a plot ratio of 3:1 will restrict the floor area of a new building to three times the area of its site (see Fig. 1.1). One of the principal reasons for the

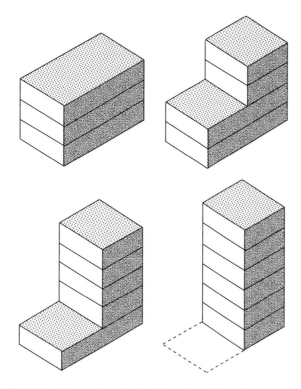

Fig. 1.1 Alternative designs for a site with a plot ratio of 3:1

introduction of plot ratio control was to restrict the heights, scale and mass of buildings in towns and cities so as not to impair the amenity and development possibilities of surrounding sites and buildings. Without this form of control, buildings could completely fill their sites with the likelihood that taller buildings would cut out daylight from their neighbours, turning streets into 'canyons' of building facades – a feature commonly seen in cities in the USA.

Plot ratio control is used by different planning authorities on an *ad hoc* basis to suit their own requirements and is most likely to be applied in the central areas of large towns and cities, where plot ratios are often restricted to between 3:1 and 5:1.

The application of plot ratio control in restricting the size of new developments often makes it advantageous to refurbish existing buildings, rather than to demolish and replace them. For example, most Victorian buildings were built to much higher plot ratios than is currently permitted by planners, some having a plot ratio of 7:1 in areas where plot ratios for new developments may well be restricted to 3:1 or 4:1. It is therefore clear that the refurbishment of such a building, retaining its existing relatively high plot ratio, could result in the provision of around twice as much 'new' floor space as

would be permitted if it were to be demolished and replaced with a new building. In such cases, where current plot ratios would prove restrictive, and where the existing building is suitable for adaptation to provide the accommodation the developer requires, it is usually well worth while giving serious consideration to opting for refurbishment rather than demolition and new construction.

1.9 Listed building legislation

Section 1 of the Planning (Listed Buildings and Conservation Areas) Act 1990 requires the Secretary of State for the Environment to compile lists of buildings of special architectural or historic interest in order that they can be protected from demolition or insensitive alteration and, therefore, preserved for the enjoyment of present and future generations. When a building has been included in the list of buildings of special architectural or historic interest it is an offence, under the provisions of the Act, to carry out works of complete or partial demolition, alteration or extension in any manner which would affect its character without first having obtained listed building consent from the local planning authority. In considering whether or not to grant listed building consent, the local planning authority must consult specified national conservation bodies, and take into account any representations made by other interested parties including local conservation groups, together with its own internal professional conservation officers.

The detailed requirements with regard to listed buildings are contained in the Town and Country Planning (Listed Buildings and Buildings in Conservation Areas) Regulations 1990, and comprehensive guidance is given in the Department of the Environment *Planning and the Historic Environment* (PPG 15) 1994.

The number of listed buildings in Great Britain is in the region of half a million and it is quite likely, therefore, especially in older towns and cities, that a 'developable' building might be listed, and this will almost certainly rule out the possibility of total demolition which is only very rarely permitted. However, it is possible, in the majority of cases, to carry out 'sensitive' refurbishment and alteration (including partial demolition and/or extension) of listed buildings, provided that those features for which the building was listed are retained.

Generally, the extent of alteration permitted will depend on the grade of listing; for example, the majority (96%) of listed buildings are Grade II, many of which possess only external features worthy of retention, such as the principal street facade, or possibly the entire external envelope of an isolated building. In such cases it may be possible to go as far as replacing the entire interior with a new structure, with only the external elevation(s), which led to the listing of the building, being retained. On the other hand, if the building has a Grade I listing (2% of all listed buildings), any possible alterations will be severely limited since Grade I listed buildings are of exceptional interest and usually possess both interior and exterior features which must be retained.

It is clear, therefore, where a listed building is the subject of a proposed development, that the developer will be restricted to the refurbishment option within the constraints imposed by its listing, although, as has been stated, in many cases it may be permissible to carry out a considerable amount of reconstruction behind the retained external elevations. On the other hand, if the design constraints imposed by the building's listing are too great, the developer will be left with no choice but to find a different site or another building.

1.10 Conservation area legislation

Section 69 of the Planning (Listed Buildings and Conservation Areas) Act 1990 requires local authorities to determine whether there are any areas within their jurisdiction which are of special architectural or historic interest, the character or appearance of which it is desirable to preserve or enhance, and to designate those areas as conservation areas. Conservation areas may be large or small, from whole town centres to squares, terraces and smaller groups of buildings. Local authorities must then pay special attention to the desirability of preserving or enhancing the character and appearance of conservation areas within their jurisdiction. The Planning (Listed Buildings and Conservation Areas) Act 1990 brings the demolition (deemed also to include partial demolition) of buildings within conservation areas, whether listed or not, under control by applying, with modifications, the listed building control provisions of the Act. Any developer wishing to demolish (or partially demolish) an unlisted building within a conservation area must first apply to the local authority for

conservation area consent, following which similar procedures to those involving listed buildings are put into effect.

It is clear, therefore, that in executing its responsibilities of preserving or enhancing the character or appearance of conservation areas, the local planning authority may impose strict constraints on the proposed development of all buildings within conservation areas whether or not they have been listed. In most cases this will rule out the possibility of total demolition and redevelopment and it is also unlikely that any alterations to a building will be permitted if they are likely to detract from the appearance or character of the conservation area.

Many 'developable' buildings, whilst they may not be listed, stand in conservation areas and, as has been stated, if these buildings form an essential part of the area's character and appearance, the development possibilities will be limited. It is therefore essential that the developer establishes what design constraints are likely to be imposed on any proposed refurbishment scheme as early as possible, since these may well be a key factor in determining whether or not it is worth while going any further in examining the feasibility of the scheme. Generally, however, it will usually be possible to go further in partially demolishing, altering or extending an unlisted building in a conservation area than would be possible with a listed building, where the design constraints are likely to be much more stringent.

1.11 The architectural advantages

There are often architectural advantages, which can be translated into financial advantages, in keeping attractive, usually older, buildings, and refurbishing them to provide modern accommodation. Many older buildings possess far greater character than their modern counterparts, incorporating skilled craftsmanship and high-quality natural materials in their design and construction. Such buildings are often more attractive to certain users such as banks, insurance companies and other financial institutions as well as commercial organisations, many of which like to project a prestigious image to their customers which is often associated with older, architecturally attractive buildings. In addition, many such buildings stand in areas where they are in close proximity to other architecturally attractive old buildings, and this adds further to their appeal and potential value, provided that their refurbishment maintains their architectural character and integrity.

1.12   Availability of the existing infrastructure

Certain refurbishment schemes can benefit from the retention and re-use of existing infrastructure, giving, in turn, further financial savings which would not be gained if the demolition and newbuild option were chosen. A common example of this is the refurbishment of large, run-down housing estates in preference to their demolition and replacement with new housing. Substantial financial savings are achieved since, not only are the houses themselves re-used, but also the existing 'housing infrastructure' including roads, drainage, gas, electricity and water supplies, telecommunications, cable networks and other utility services – all, or most, of which would have to be completely renewed if the demolition and new build option were chosen. There are many other examples where infrastructure costs can be saved, and although the greatest savings will be achieved on larger-scale projects involving more than one building, infrastructure savings are also possible when individual buildings are refurbished since they will normally already have road access and be connected to most of the services mentioned above.

As well as achieving these direct financial savings, the avoidance of having to provide a new infrastructure will also reduce the development period, resulting in further indirect financial savings as discussed in Section 1.4.

1.13   The social advantages

The refurbishment of large housing estates has important sociological advantages when compared with demolition and newbuild. One of the most disruptive aspects of the comprehensive, national policies of demolition and replacement of sub-standard housing during the 1960s and early 1970s was that established communities, many of which had existed for several generations, were broken up permanently. The 'creation' of new communities has since been recognised as a complex process, and the refurbishment of existing housing, by preserving

established, stable communities, is therefore considered preferable to the alternative of wholesale clearance and new development.

1.14   The environmental advantages

A major focus of concern during the past 30 years, and one which has continued to increase in importance, is the massive worldwide consumption of energy, and its related adverse implications including global warming. One of the many ways in which worldwide energy consumption can be reduced is to recycle and re-use existing resources as much as possible, in preference to consuming even more energy by replacing them. Whenever a building is recycled by opting for refurbishment rather than newbuild, a considerable amount of energy is saved by avoiding the need to extract raw materials and convert them into a replacement building. 'Low-key' refurbishment, where most of the existing structure and fabric are retained, will clearly yield the greatest energy savings, but even the more drastic forms, where major alterations are made, will generally use less energy than demolition and newbuild.

References

Building Research Establishment (1991) *Structural Appraisal of Existing Buildings for Change of Use* (Digest 366), BRE, Watford.

Cantacuzino, S. and Brandt, S. (1980) *Saving Old Buildings*, Architectural Press, London.

Construction Industry Research and Information Association (1994) *A Guide to the Management of Building Refurbishment* (Report 133), CIRIA, London.

Corbett-Winder, K. (1995) *The Barn Book*, Random Century, London.

Davis, J., Goldsworthy, J. and Moncrieff, D. (1997) *The Directory of Grant Making Trusts*, 15th edn, Vols 1 and 2, Charities Aid Foundation, West Malling, Kent.

Department of the Environment (1994) *Planning and the Historic Environment* (Planning Policy Guidance 15), HMSO, London.

Department of the Environment (1996) *English House Condition Survey 1996*, HMSO, London.

Great Britain (1987) *Town and Country Planning (Use Classes) Order 1987*, HMSO, London.

Great Britain (1990) *Planning (Listed Buildings and Conservation Areas) Regulations 1990* (Statutory Instruments, no. 1519), HMSO, London.

Great Britain (1990) *Town and Country Planning Act 1990*, ch. 8, HMSO, London.

Great Britain (1990) *Planning (Listed Buildings and Conservation Areas) Act 1990*, ch. 9, HMSO, London.

Great Britain (1991) *Town and Country Planning (Use Classes) Amendment Order 1991*, HMSO, London.

Pickard, R.D. (1996) *Conservation in the Built Environment*, Longman, London.

Pollard, R. (1998) 'Redundant Government Buildings', *The Building Conservation Directory 1998*, ed. J. Taylor, Cathedral Communications Ltd., Tisbury, 25–7.

2

Upgrading the fire-resistance of existing elements

2.1 General

Any refurbishment scheme, especially if it involves a building containing exposed structural elements of timber, steel or iron, is likely to need some upgrading of fire-resistance if it is to comply with current regulations. Generally, the older the building, the more likely it will be to require fire upgrading owing to the nature of its construction, a typical example being a nineteenth-century docklands warehouse being converted into offices. Many buildings of this type and period have open joisted timber floors supported by exposed wrought-iron beams and cast-iron columns, none of which would come near to complying with current fire regulations. The timber roof structures of such buildings, often left exposed from below, and their timber staircases would also require upgrading. Another example, on a smaller scale, might be the conversion of a large Victorian house into flats. Here, the fire-resistance of the existing timber stairs and the floors which would separate the newly created flats would, as existing, not comply with current fire regulations for the proposed new use and would therefore need upgrading.

2.2 Statutory requirements

Most refurbished buildings, including those involving alterations, extensions or a change of use, must comply with the Building Regulations, and one of the most important sections affecting refurbishment schemes is Part B3: Internal Fire Spread (Structure). Compliance with Part B3 will almost certainly involve upgrading the fire-resistance of some existing elements of structure or replacing them with new construction, and, in older buildings with many exposed timber, iron and steel elements, the upgrading work and associated costs can be considerable.

To comply with Regulation B3, the designer of the building can use the non-mandatory guidance contained in *Approved Document B: Fire Safety*, or use alternative ways of demonstrating compliance provided the chosen solution is adequate to meet the requirements of the Regulations. Regulation B3 requires that loadbearing elements of structure, such as columns, beams, floors and walls, must have at least the fire-resistance given in the tables contained in *Approved Document B* to the Regulations. The tables give required minimum periods of fire-resistance from half an hour to four hours, depending on the purpose group of the building and its height and size. (The purpose group is a means of classifying a building according to the hazard to life that a fire would present, which is determined partly by the building's use. Buildings containing sleeping accommodation or aged or infirm people, for example, are regarded as particularly hazardous and, as a result, have more stringent requirements with regard to fire protection than, say, buildings used for the storage of goods.)

2.3 Fire-resistance of elements

Approved Document B to the Building Regulations specifies the required fire-resistance of elements in terms of the results they achieve when subjected to standardised fire tests. The procedures for the tests, which must be carried out on properly made-up specimens of the constructions being evaluated under strictly controlled conditions, are laid down in the various parts of British Standard 476. The fire-resistance tests for structural (loadbearing) elements of construction, including columns, beams, floors and walls, are contained in BS 476: Part 21: 1987 (*Methods for Determination of the Fire-resistance of Load-bearing Elements of Construction*). It should be noted that fire-resistance in the contexts of both new construction and refurbishment is not a characteristic of a material, but the performance of a complete element of construction which will normally comprise a number of different materials and components. Fire-resistance is therefore determined in a test which subjects a representative specimen to heating which simulates its anticipated exposure in a real building fire, for example floors from below, walls from one side and columns on all sides. Loadbearing elements are subjected to their design loadings during the tests. The fire-resistance of the specimen is the time in minutes for which it continues to meet whichever of the following criteria are relevant:

- Loadbearing capacity: applicable only to loadbearing elements. Failure occurs when the test specimen can no longer support its design loading. For horizontal elements (e.g., floors and beams), limits are specified for the allowable extent of vertical deflection.

- Integrity: applicable only to elements that separate spaces (e.g., walls and floors). Failure occurs when the specimen collapses, exhibits sustained flaming on its unexposed face, or when cracks or other openings form through which flame or hot gases can pass.

- Insulation: applicable only to elements that separate spaces. Failure occurs when the temperature of the unexposed (to fire) face of the element increases by more than 140 degrees C above the initial temperature, or by more than 180 degrees C, regardless of the initial temperature.

The two most common fire-resistance upgrading requirements in refurbishment work involve timber floors and unprotected beams and columns of steel or, in older buildings, cast iron.

2.4 Upgrading the fire-resistance of timber floors

One of the most common examples where the upgrading of existing timber floors proves necessary is in the refurbishment and conversion to modern use of the numerous old, often redundant, factory and warehouse buildings constructed between 1850 and 1920. Such buildings are abundant in towns and cities and therefore form a large proportion of those that lend themselves to refurbishment and adaptation to modern uses, especially as many are located in prime development areas such as river and canal sides and docklands. Typical new uses include flats, maisonettes, offices, restaurants, shops and museums, and in all cases their original timber floors will almost certainly require their fire-resistance upgraded to comply with current regulations. In the majority of these utilitarian industrial buildings, the undersides of floors did not receive a ceiling finish and merely comprised floorboarding on timber joists left exposed on the underside. In addition, many such floors have plain-edge boarding which is often found to have distorted over the years, leaving gaps between them which, in the absence of a ceiling beneath, render the floor almost totally ineffective as a fire barrier since the floor would have minimal or zero integrity (see fire-resistance criteria, Section 2.3). Timber floors of this type come nowhere near to meeting the fire-resistance standards required by modern regulations and therefore require extensive upgrading, in most cases to either half an hour or one hour depending on the purpose group, height and size of the building.

Another common example where upgrading of existing timber floors proves necessary is the conversion of large single dwellings into self-contained flats or maisonettes. Here, the focus for attention is the floors that will separate the newly created occupancies and these will need to be upgraded to half-hour fire-resistance in two-storey buildings and one-hour fire-resistance in buildings of three or more storeys. In all cases, any floor over a basement storey must have one-hour fire-resistance. Where an existing dwelling is being converted, it is clear that the floors requiring upgrading will already have some form of ceiling finish providing some degree of fire-resistance and generally the upgrading treatment will not need to be as extensive as industrial-type floors with exposed joists. However, it should be noted that a typical floor construction of plain-edge boards and a lath and plaster ceiling, often found in older buildings, will still need an upgrading treatment even if it has to achieve only a half-hour fire-resistance after conversion.

The most common technique used to upgrade the fire-resistance of existing timber floors is to add a new fire-resisting layer beneath the existing joists or ceiling. This may also involve the insertion of a layer of fire-resisting material within the void, resting on the new ceiling. In certain cases, however, it may not be acceptable to cover the existing ceiling with a new layer, and in such cases an alternative technique may be used which involves filling the void between the existing floor surface and ceiling with a fire-resisting material. Both techniques are described in detail below.

2.4.1 Addition of a new fire-resisting layer beneath the existing joists or ceiling

A wide range of techniques and materials are available for use in upgrading the fire-resistance of existing timber floors. Most, as previously stated, involve providing either a completely new ceiling where originally the joists were

exposed, or an extra layer to the underside of the existing ceiling. In some cases it may also be necessary to provide an additional layer of fire-resisting material on top of the existing floorboards or between the floor joists. Typical practical upgrading techniques for a variety of existing floor constructions are given in Tables 2.1–2.4 and illustrated in Figs. 2.1–2.4, indicating the fire-resistances that can be achieved. Several of the techniques involve the use of proprietary materials, descriptions of which are given below.

> It should be noted that the upgrading techniques and specifications are provided for guidance only, and that the product manufacturers should be consulted for detailed specifications and instructions.

2.4.1.1 Supalux and Masterboard

Description: A rigid board, developed to replace asbestos-based products, consisting of a hydrated calcium-silicate matrix reinforced with special cellulose fibres and inorganic additives, cured in high-pressure steam autoclaves.

Table 2.1 Treatments for upgrading the fire-resistance of an existing floor construction of plain-edge floorboards 22mm thick on timber joists not less than 38mm thick; no ceiling

Upgrading treatment	Resulting fire-resistance
1 Expanded metal lathing nailed to joists with gypsum plaster finish 16mm thick	½ hour
2* Expanded metal lathing nailed to joists with vermiculite-gypsum plaster finish 12.5mm thick	½ hour
3* Plasterboard 12.5mm thick nailed to joists with gypsum plaster finish 12.5mm thick	½ hour
4 2 layers of plasterboard nailed to joists with joints staggered, total thickness 25mm	½ hour
5* Hardboard sheet 3mm thick nailed to floorboards. Masterboard 6mm thick nailed to joists	½ hour
6* Hardboard sheet 3mm thick nailed to floorboards. Supalux boards 9mm thick screwed to joists through 80mm × 9mm Supalux fillets and overlaid with 60mm mineral wool mat (density 23 kg/m^3)	1 hour
7* Hardboard sheet 3mm thick nailed to floorboards. New Tacfire boards 9mm thick nailed or screwed to joists through 75 × 9mm New Tacfire cover fillets, and overlaid with 40mm rock wool mat (density 60 kg/m^3)	1 hour

* See Fig. 2.1

Table 2.2 Treatments for upgrading the fire-resistance of an existing floor construction of tongued and grooved floorboards not less than 19mm thick on timber joists not less than 38mm thick; no ceiling

Upgrading treatment	Resulting fire-resistance
1 Expanded metal lathing nailed to joists with gypsum plaster finish 16mm thick	½ hour
2 Plasterboard 9.5mm thick nailed to joists with gypsum plaster finish 12.5mm thick	½ hour
3* Plasterboard 12.5mm thick nailed to joists with gypsum plaster finish 5mm thick	½ hour
4* 2 layers of plasterboard nailed to joists with joints staggered, total thickness 22mm	½ hour
5* Masterboard 6mm thick nailed to joists	½ hour
6 Expanded metal lathing nailed to joists with gypsum plaster finish 22mm thick	1 hour
7* Expanded metal lathing nailed to joists with vermiculite-gypsum plaster finish 12.5mm thick	1 hour
8 Plasterboard 9.5mm thick nailed to joists with vermiculite-gypsum plaster finish 12.5mm thick	1 hour
9* Supalux board 9mm thick screwed to joists through 80mm × 9mm Supalux fillets and overlaid with 60mm mineral wool mat (density 23 kg/m³)	1 hour

* See Fig. 2.2

Sizes and thicknesses: 1220–3050mm long × 610 or 1220mm wide × 6, 9, 12, 15 or 20mm thick.

Decoration: Boards can be tightly butt-jointed or their edges left slightly apart for filling and sanding. The boards do not require any surface treatment to attain their stated fire-resistance and painting does not alter fire-resistance. Suitable finishes include paint, paper, tiles or plaster.

2.4.1.2 New Tacfire

Description: A rigid, autoclaved calcium-silicate board material with a smooth upper surface which is off-white in colour. Fixed to timber by nailing or screwing.

Sizes and thicknesses: Four standard sizes from 2134 to 3000mm long × 914 to 1250mm wide (other sizes available). Six standard thicknesses from 6 to 25mm.

Decoration: New Tacfire can be painted, papered, tiled (on minimum 9mm thick boards), or finished with a proprietary decorative coating such as Artex.

2.4.1.3 Sprayed Limpet Mineral Wool – GP Grade

Description: A blend of mineral wool and selected inorganic fillers and binders applied by spraying to form a homogeneous jointless coating.

Finishing/Decoration: Can be left either as sprayed or with a tamped, stippled finish which can be coated with Limpet LD3 – a white decorative finish. This can, if required, be overpainted.

2.4.1.4 Intumescent materials

Intumescent materials are applied to surfaces in very thin coatings which, when exposed to fire, undergo a chemical reaction which protects the material to which they have been applied from intense heat. (A more detailed description is given in Section 2.5.4.) Nullifire System W is a proprietary intumescent material designed specifically for upgrading the fire-resistance of timber elements. The waterborne intumescent coating has a high flame-retardant content which provides spread of flame protection to natural timber surfaces, delaying the onset

Table 2.3 Treatments for upgrading the fire-resistance of an existing floor construction of tongued and grooved floorboards not less than 22mm thick on timber joists not less than 175 × 50mm; no ceiling

Upgrading treatment	Resulting fire-resistance
1 Expanded metal lathing nailed to joists with gypsum plaster finish 16mm thick	½ hour
2* Expanded metal lathing nailed to joists with sprayed Limpet Mineral Wool – GP Grade finish 13mm thick	½ hour
3* Plasterboard 9.5mm thick nailed to joists with gypsum plaster finish 12.5mm thick	½ hour
4 Plasterboard 12.5mm thick nailed to joists with gypsum plaster finish 5mm thick	½ hour
5 2 layers of plasterboard nailed to joists with joints staggered, total thickness 19mm	½ hour
6* Expanded metal lathing nailed to joists with sprayed Limpet Mineral Wool – GP Grade finish 22mm thick	1 hour
7* Plasterboard 9.5mm thick nailed to joists with vermiculite-gypsum plaster finish 12.5mm thick	1 hour
8* Supalux board 9mm thick screwed to joists through 80mm × 9mm Supalux fillets and overlaid with 60mm mineral wool mat (density 23 kg/m^3)	1 hour
9 New Tacfire boards 9mm thick nailed or screwed to joists through 75 × 9mm New Tacfire cover fillets, and overlaid with 40mm rock wool mat (density 60 kg/m^3)	1 hour

* See Fig. 2.3

Table 2.4 Treatments for upgrading the fire-resistance of an existing floor construction of plain-edge floorboards, 22mm thick on timber joists not less than 50mm thick; wood lath and plaster ceiling 16mm thick

Upgrading treatment	Resulting fire-resistance
1* Plasterboard 12.5mm thick nailed to joists through existing ceiling	½ hour
2* Hardboard sheet 3mm thick nailed to floorboards. Two Supalux strips 9mm thick × 50mm deep fixed to each side of joists with nails. 12mm Supalux boards laid on top of support strips	½ hour
3* Plasterboard 9.5mm thick nailed to joists through existing ceiling with gypsum plaster finish 9mm thick	1 hour
4* Hardboard sheet 4.8mm thick nailed to floorboards. Supalux board 12mm thick screwed to joists through existing ceiling	1 hour

* See Fig. 2.4

Existing floor construction: Plain edge floorboards 22mm thick on timber joists not less than 38mm thick. No ceiling.		
Detail	Upgrading Treatment	Fire-resistance
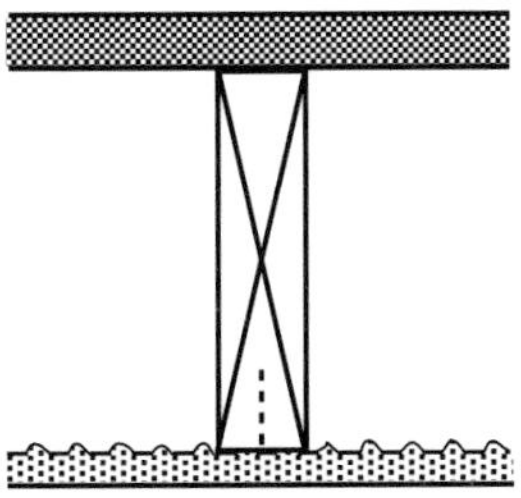	Expanded metal lathing nailed to joists with vermiculite gypsum plaster finish 12.5mm thick	½ Hour
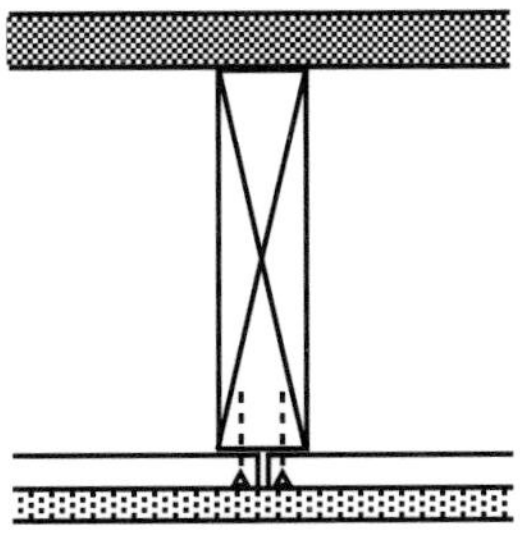	Plasterboard 12.5mm thick nailed to joists with gypsum plaster finish 12.5mm thick	½ Hour
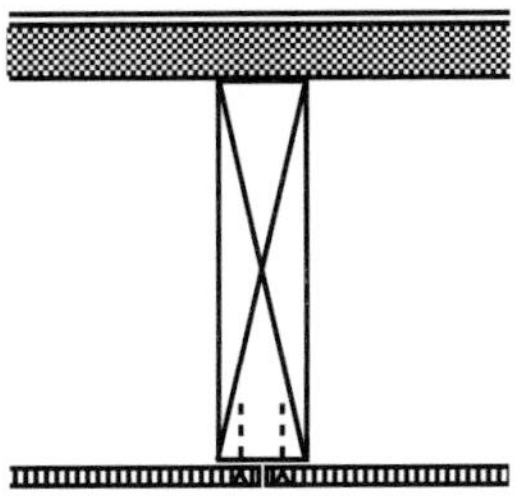	Hardboard sheet 3mm thick nailed to floorboards Masterboard 6mm thick nailed to joists	½ Hour
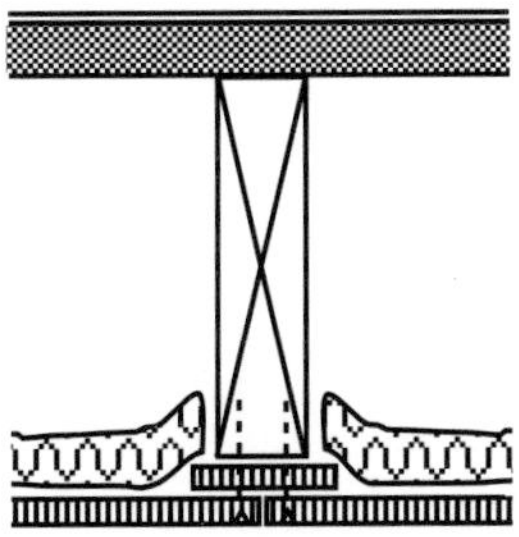	Hardboard sheet 3mm thick nailed to floorboards Supalux board 9mm thick screwed to joists through 80mm x 9mm thick Supalux fillet overlaid with 60mm mineral wool mat (density 23kg/m³)	1 Hour
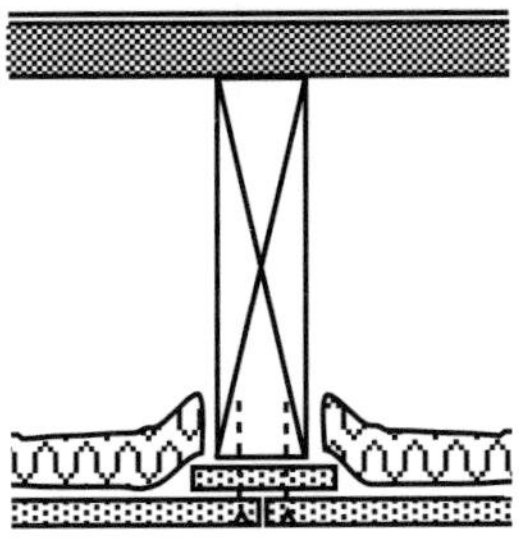	Hardboard sheet 3mm thick nailed to floorboards New Tacfire board 9mm thick nailed or screwed to joists through 75x9mm New Tacfire cover fillets and overlaid with 40mm rock wool mat (density 60kg/m³)	1 Hour

Fig. 2.1 Upgrading the fire-resistance of timber floors

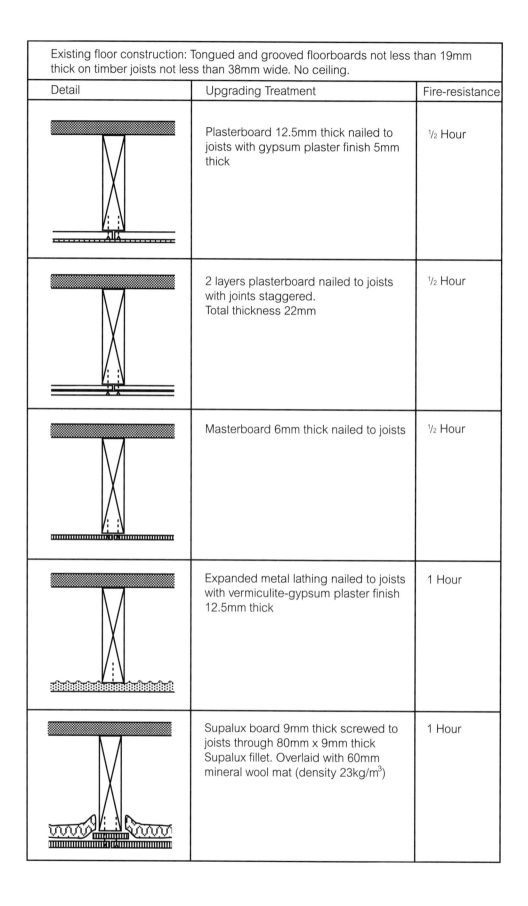

Existing floor construction: Tongued and grooved floorboards not less than 19mm thick on timber joists not less than 38mm wide. No ceiling.		
Detail	Upgrading Treatment	Fire-resistance
	Plasterboard 12.5mm thick nailed to joists with gypsum plaster finish 5mm thick	½ Hour
	2 layers plasterboard nailed to joists with joints staggered. Total thickness 22mm	½ Hour
	Masterboard 6mm thick nailed to joists	½ Hour
	Expanded metal lathing nailed to joists with vermiculite-gypsum plaster finish 12.5mm thick	1 Hour
	Supalux board 9mm thick screwed to joists through 80mm x 9mm thick Supalux fillet. Overlaid with 60mm mineral wool mat (density 23kg/m^3)	1 Hour

Fig. 2.2 Upgrading the fire-resistance of timber floors

Detail	Upgrading Treatment	Fire-resistance
Existing floor construction: Tongued and grooved floorboards not less than 22mm thick on timber joists not less than 175mm x 50mm. No ceiling.		
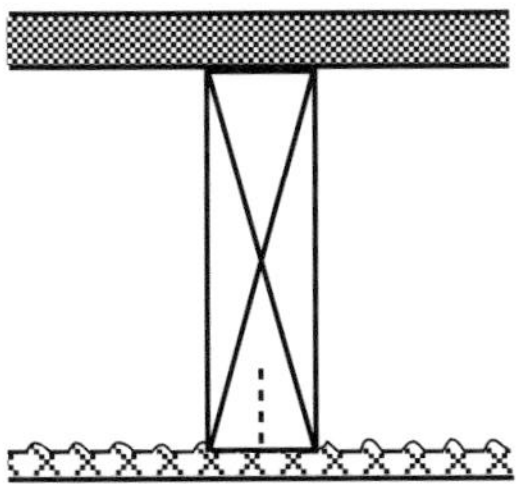	Expanded metal lathing nailed to joists with Sprayed Limpet Mineral Wool - GP Grade finish 13mm thick	½ Hour
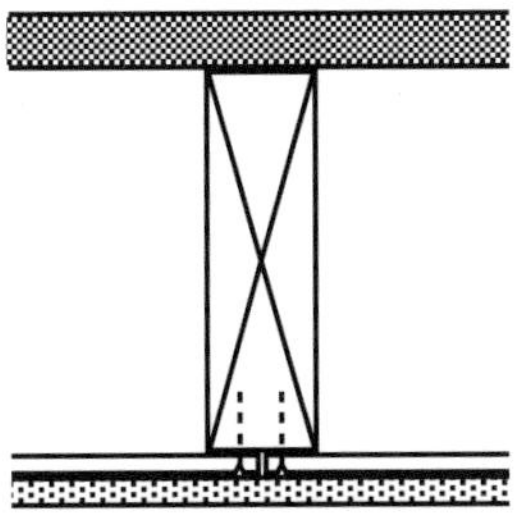	Plasterboard 9.5mm thick nailed to joists with gypsum plaster finish 12.5mm thick	½ Hour
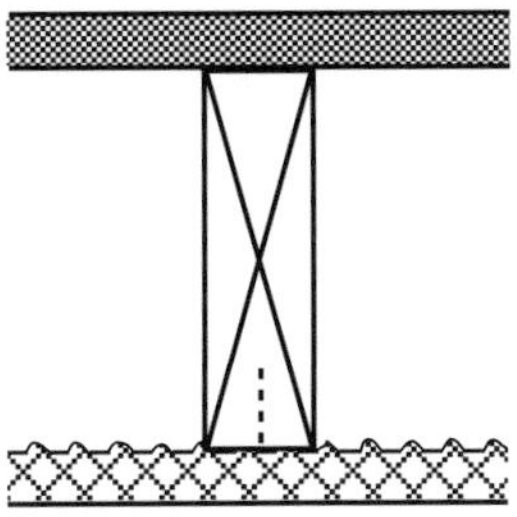	Expanded metal lathing nailed to joists with Sprayed Limpet Mineral Wool - GP Grade finish 22mm thick	1 Hour
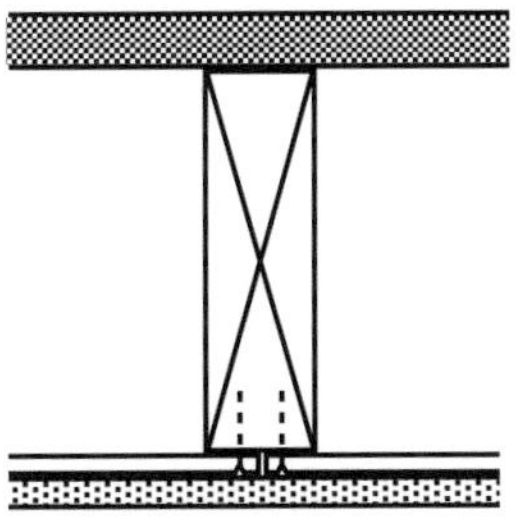	Plasterboard 9.5mm thick nailed to joists with vermiculite gypsum plaster finish 12.5mm thick	1 Hour
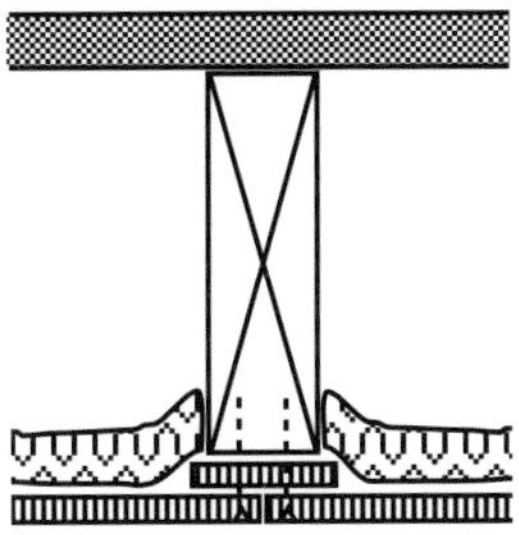	Supalux board 9mm thick screwed to joists through 80mm x 9mm Supalux fillets. Overlaid with 60mm mineral wool mat (density 23kg/m^3)	1 Hour

Fig. 2.3   Upgrading the fire-resistance of timber floors

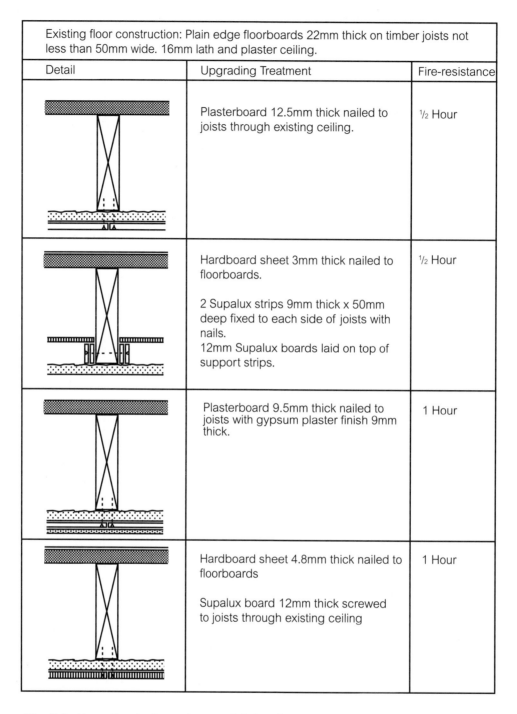

Existing floor construction: Plain edge floorboards 22mm thick on timber joists not less than 50mm wide. 16mm lath and plaster ceiling.		
Detail	Upgrading Treatment	Fire-resistance
	Plasterboard 12.5mm thick nailed to joists through existing ceiling.	½ Hour
	Hardboard sheet 3mm thick nailed to floorboards. 2 Supalux strips 9mm thick x 50mm deep fixed to each side of joists with nails. 12mm Supalux boards laid on top of support strips.	½ Hour
	Plasterboard 9.5mm thick nailed to joists with gypsum plaster finish 9mm thick.	1 Hour
	Hardboard sheet 4.8mm thick nailed to floorboards Supalux board 12mm thick screwed to joists through existing ceiling	1 Hour

Fig. 2.4   Upgrading the fire-resistance of timber floors

of charring of the timber by an average of 17 minutes. This delay effectively increases the inherent fire-resistance of the timber and it is possible to upgrade existing timber floors with exposed joists to half-hour fire-resistance provided the existing timber is of adequate thickness. Nullifire System W consists of an intumescent basecoat and a topseal applied by brush, roller or spray, with a total thickness of less than 1mm, enabling the profile and character of the existing timbers, including joists, panelling and mouldings, to be preserved in refurbishment work. The topseal may be clear (matt or satin), if the natural appearance of the timber is to be preserved, or pigmented in any of the full BS 4800 colour range, if a decorative finish is required.

2.4.2 Insertion of a new fire-resisting material into the void between the existing floorboards and ceiling

The key feature of the methods described in Section 2.4.1, above, is that where a ceiling finish already exists, it will be covered, and therefore concealed, by the new fire-resisting layer applied to its underside. It is quite likely, particularly in older buildings which have been listed as being of historic or architectural importance, that some ceilings may themselves be protected from alteration, for example if they comprise ornate historic plasterwork. In such cases, upgrading of fire-resistance by the addition of a new layer beneath the existing ceiling would not be permitted under any circumstances and, therefore, some other upgrading technique would have to be employed. The addition of a fire-resisting layer to the floor surface above the ceiling is generally inappropriate as the main protection should be to that part of the floor structure beneath the floorboards, and thus, the only means of providing the required fire-resistance is by inserting a new fire-resisting material into the void between the existing floorboards and ornate ceiling.

A proprietary material specifically developed for this purpose is Tilcon Foamed Perlite. This is a site-mixed material, produced from expanded perlite lightweight aggregate, a water-based aerated foam, inorganic hydraulic binders and special additives, which can be pumped into the floor void to upgrade the fire-resistance of existing timber floors. The material is produced on site using a suitable mixer and foam generator, and pump-injected directly into the void after removing selected floorboards. The foamed perlite, which sets and cures to a solid light-grey honeycombed matrix, bonds itself to the sides of the joists and is further held in place by metal brackets.

Official fire tests have shown that existing lath and plaster ceilings, even where they have heavy ornate mouldings, give less than half-an-hour fire-resistance. The insertion of Tilcon Foamed Perlite into the floor cavity, to a depth of 175mm, will increase the fire-resistance of such a floor to one hour (loadbearing capacity, integrity and insulation). The upgrading of an existing timber floor using this technique is illustrated in Fig. 2.5.

Foamed perlite can, of course, be used to upgrade any type of timber floor with a fillable void between the floor surface and ceiling, and the material can also be used for a range of other fire-resisting applications. Further

advantages of this method are that scaffolding access to the underside of existing floors, needed with other methods, is not required, and existing light fittings are not disturbed.

2.5 Upgrading the fire-resistance of wrought-iron, cast-iron and steel elements

Although wrought and cast iron and steel are non-combustible materials, they are at least as vulnerable as timber to building fires; indeed large-section timber beams are often better at withstanding fire thanks to natural, protective sacrificial charring of their outer layers which offers protection from further damage. Wrought and cast iron and steel, whilst being incombustible, are, nevertheless, highly vulnerable to fire, sustaining considerable strength loss and distortion at relatively low temperatures in the evolution of a typical building fire. It should also be noted that wrought and cast iron are less predictable than steel when exposed to fire because of their inherent susceptibility to cracking.

As stated in Section 2.1, large numbers of old buildings that are suitable for refurbishment and alteration contain exposed structural beams and columns of iron or steel, and it is often convenient and economical, particularly in the lower-key categories of refurbishment, to retain these elements. However, as with timber floor structures, the fire-resistance of exposed iron and steel work does not approach the standards that are required today and some form of upgrading will therefore be necessary. In many of our older industrial buildings, structural frames comprising ornate, circular cast-iron columns and wrought-iron main beams support timber secondary beams and floorboarding, and it is often desirable to retain the shape and form of the existing columns as an architectural feature in the refurbished building. In such cases, the materials used in upgrading fire-resistance must be capable of application in the form of a very thin coating if the shape and form of the existing sections are to be preserved.

A wide range of techniques and materials are available for upgrading the fire-resistance of exposed iron and steel structural elements and all of them are suitable for 'I'-section beams and columns. The techniques available for upgrading circular columns, however, are more limited, since some of the materials used are

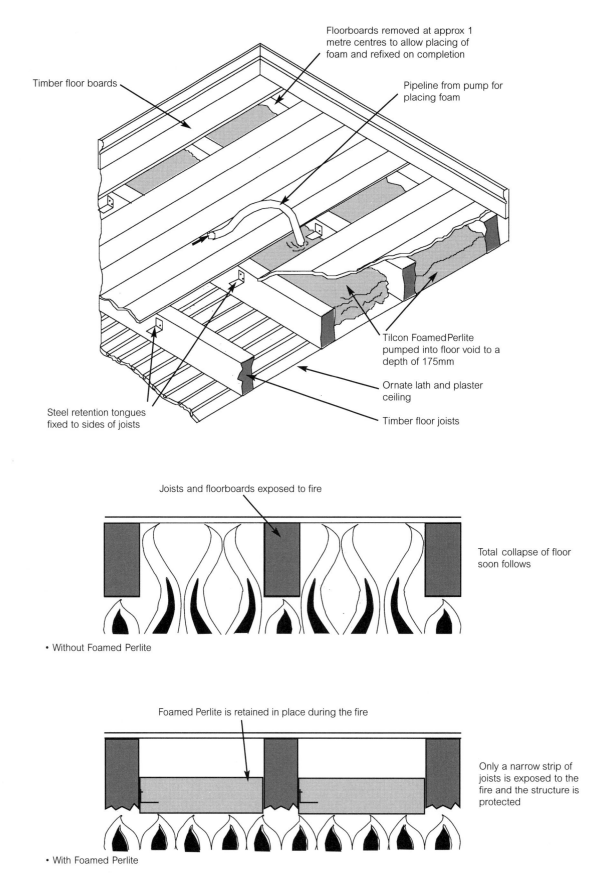

Fig. 2.5 Upgrading the fire-resistance of timber floors

not capable of being applied to circular sections. The techniques and materials used vary considerably in their application and use and fall into four basic categories which are described below, and illustrated in Figs. 2.6 and 2.7.

It should be noted that the upgrading techniques and specifications are provided for guidance only, and that the product manufacturers should be consulted for detailed specifications and instructions.

The figures give the fire-resistances that can be achieved for various thicknesses of protection, but it should be noted that the data are only approximate and intended to be an indication of requirements for sections of 'typical size' ('I' sections: 406mm × 178mm × 74 kg/m; circular sections: 190mm diameter × 8mm thick). In practice, the actual thickness of protection required will vary and is based on the ratio of the section's exposed surface area to the area of its cross-section. The higher the surface area for a given cross-sectional area, the more heat will be absorbed and thus the lower the inherent fire-resistance of the section. The actual thickness of the protection required will therefore increase as the ratio of surface area to cross-sectional area increases, and it is necessary to refer to manufacturers' tables, or to use calculations, in order to arrive at the actual thickness of protection required for any particular section. It should also be noted that the thickness of fire protection required for beams is usually less than that required for columns because beams are exposed to fire only on three sides whereas columns are normally exposed on all four sides; this is applicable only where the top flange of the beam is protected by a dense concrete floor slab of at least 100mm thick.

2.5.1 Solid encasement

Although other materials can be used, solid encasement normally involves casting in-situ concrete around the sections being upgraded. To obtain a good bond between the concrete and the steel or iron elements, steel mesh wrapping fabric is applied to the sections before erecting the temporary formwork and pouring the concrete. The minimum concrete cover to sections being protected must be 25mm to allow for the maximum coarse aggregate size, and this will give two hours fire-resistance to any steel or cast-iron section. Good-quality control in the production of the concrete is essential since its performance in fire can vary considerably depending on its density, moisture content and the aggregates used.

When considering the use of in-situ concrete to upgrade existing cast-iron and steel elements, it should be borne in mind that it is a messy operation, and that erection of temporary formwork within the existing building, together with the provision of adequate access into the building for the mixed concrete, may cause considerable difficulties.

2.5.2 Lightweight hollow encasement

Hollow encasement techniques essentially involve 'boxing-in' the columns or beams being upgraded, with fire-resisting materials of various types. Several different materials are available, and a number of them are described below.

2.5.2.1 Expanded metal lathing and plaster

Expanded metal lathing is wrapped around the column or beam to form the key for a wet plaster finish. The lathing can be fixed to the steel section using wire clips or steel stirrups, or by spot-welding. With 'I'-section columns it is advisable to fix metal angle beads at the arrises to provide additional protection against mechanical damage. Where this method is used for circular columns, the metal lathing follows the column profile and the protection does not, therefore, form a hollow casing (see Fig. 2.6). Fire-resistances of up to one and a half hours can easily be obtained using this method, and the thickness of plaster required can be reduced if lightweight vermiculite-gypsum plaster is used. The fire-resistances obtainable using this method are given in Fig. 2.6.

2.5.2.2 Plasterboard encasement

This was the first material to be used for lightweight hollow encasement and it is still by no means uncommon in upgrading work. Lengths of 9.5mm thick plasterboard are cut to size and fixed to the steel sections by means of special metal flange clips. The plasterboard is then finished with a single coat of wet plaster, its thickness

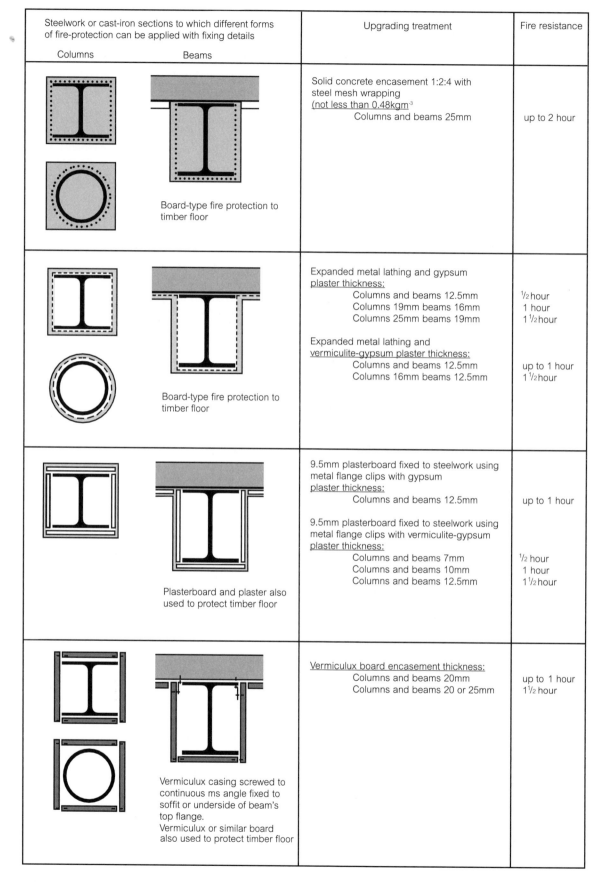

Steelwork or cast-iron sections to which different forms of fire-protection can be applied with fixing details	Upgrading treatment	Fire resistance
Columns Beams		
Board-type fire protection to timber floor	Solid concrete encasement 1:2:4 with steel mesh wrapping (not less than 0.48kgm^{-3}) 　　　　　Columns and beams 25mm	up to 2 hour
Board-type fire protection to timber floor	Expanded metal lathing and gypsum plaster thickness: 　　　Columns and beams 12.5mm 　　　Columns 19mm beams 16mm 　　　Columns 25mm beams 19mm Expanded metal lathing and vermiculite-gypsum plaster thickness: 　　　Columns and beams 12.5mm 　　　Columns 16mm beams 12.5mm	$^1/_2$ hour 1 hour 1 $^1/_2$ hour up to 1 hour 1 $^1/_2$ hour
Plasterboard and plaster also used to protect timber floor	9.5mm plasterboard fixed to steelwork using metal flange clips with gypsum plaster thickness: 　　　Columns and beams 12.5mm 9.5mm plasterboard fixed to steelwork using metal flange clips with vermiculite-gypsum plaster thickness: 　　　Columns and beams 7mm 　　　Columns and beams 10mm 　　　Columns and beams 12.5mm	up to 1 hour $^1/_2$ hour 1 hour 1 $^1/_2$ hour
Vermiculux casing screwed to continuous ms angle fixed to soffit or underside of beam's top flange. Vermiculux or similar board also used to protect timber floor	Vermiculux board encasement thickness: 　　　Columns and beams 20mm 　　　Columns and beams 20 or 25mm	up to 1 hour 1 $^1/_2$ hour

Fig. 2.6 Upgrading the fire-resistance of iron and steel beams and columns

Steelwork or cast-iron sections to which different forms of fire-protection can be applied with fixing details		Upgrading treatment	Fire resistance
Columns	Beams		

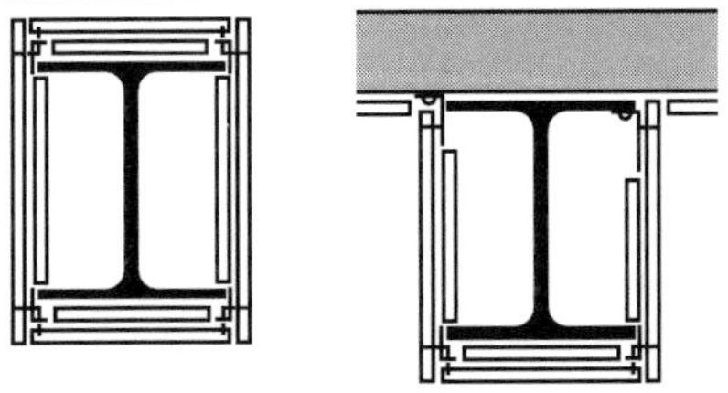 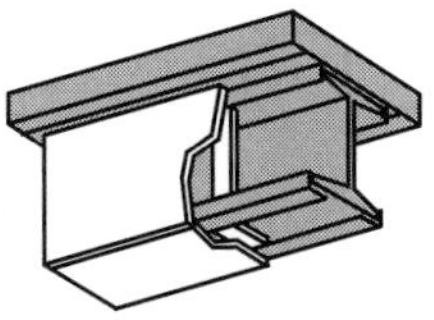
 	
 Suplax casing screwed to continuous steel angle frame-work fixed around the section. All transverse joints backed by 75mm wide suplax backing strips in same thickness as casing. Suplax board also used to protect timber floor.
		Suplalux board encasement thickness:
		     Columns and beams 6mm
		     Columns and beams 9mm
		     Columns 12mm
			$\frac{1}{2}$ hour
			 1 hour
			 $\frac{1}{2}$ hour
			 2 hour

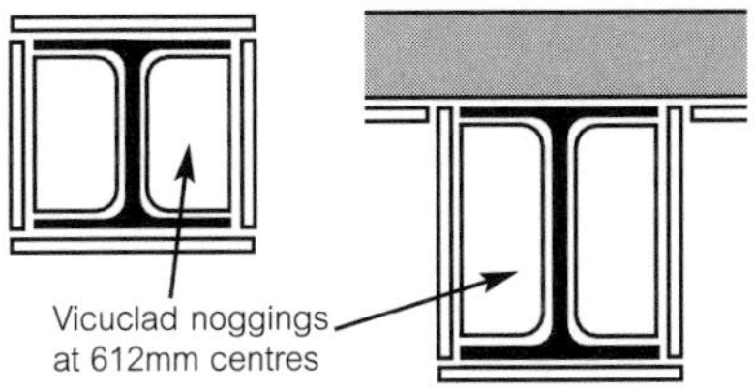
 Vicuclad noggings at 612mm centres
 Vicuclad noggings fixed behind all joints with cement into web of steel section at 612mm centres. Vicuclad casing fixed with cement to flanges and to noggings. Edge nailing using galvanised nails at all joints. Alternative fixing by screwing to steel angle fixed aound existing sections.
		Vicuclad board encasement thickness:
		     Columns and beams 18mm
		     Columns and beams 18-30mm
		     Columns and beams 30-60mm
		     Columns and beams 45-80mm
			up to 1 hour
			 $1\frac{1}{2}$ hour
			 3 hour
			 4 hour

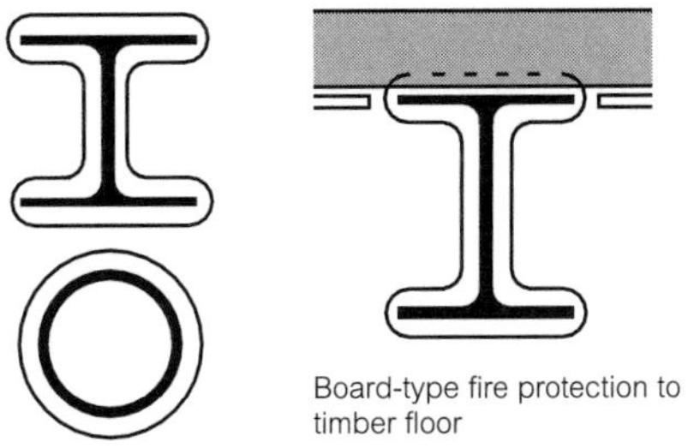
 Board-type fire protection to timber floor
		Sprayed Limpet mineral wool - GP Grade
		     Columns and beams 10mm
		     Columns and beams 12-14mm
		     Columns and beams 23-25mm
			$\frac{1}{2}$ hour
			 1 hour
			 $1\frac{1}{2}$ hour

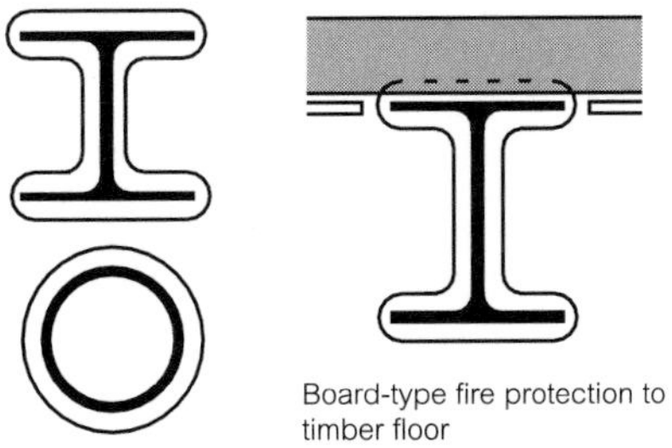
 Board-type fire protection to timber floor
		Mandolite CP2 sprayed vermiculite - cement thickness:
		     Columns and beams 8-9mm
		     Columns and beams 13-15mm
		     Columns and beams 18-20mm
			$\frac{1}{2}$ hour
			 1 hour
			 $1\frac{1}{2}$ hour

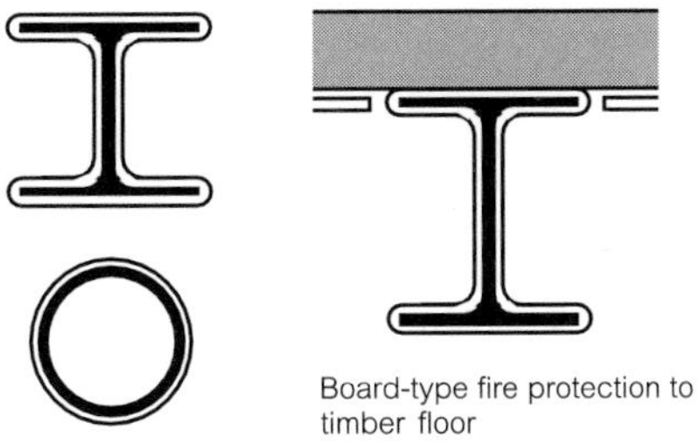
 Board-type fire protection to timber floor
		Nullifire intumescent coating applied by brush roller or spray
		     Thickness can range from 0.3mm
		     to 2.0mm dependent on HP/A
		     calculation and type of section
			$\frac{1}{2}$ hour
			 to
			 2 hour

Fig. 2.7 Upgrading the fire-resistance of iron and steel beams and columns

depending on the degree of fire-resistance required. Because of the technique used to secure the plasterboard casing to the steelwork, this method cannot be used with circular-section columns. As with the previous method, longer periods of fire-resistance can be obtained if vermiculite-gypsum plaster is used (see Fig. 2.6).

2.5.2.3 Vermiculux board encasement

Vermiculux is a proprietary, low-density board material manufactured from exfoliated vermiculite, other non-organic fibres and fillers and a calcium-silicate matrix. The boards (standard size 1220 × 610mm and 1220 × 1220mm, in thicknesses from 20 to 60mm) are cut to size on site and fixed around the steel sections by edge-screwing. Opposite edges of boards are rebated to allow lapped cross-joints to be made without the need for noggings or backing strips. Adhesives are not necessary, and the iron or steelwork needs no cleaning or priming. The completed casing can be finished (after making good countersunk screw fixings, junctions, etc., by filling and sanding) by direct painting, papering or tiling. Alternatively, a wet-skim plaster finish can be applied. Where Vermiculux is used to encase beams beneath an existing floor, it is first necessary to fix continuous mild steel angles to the soffit or beam flange by shot-firing as shown in Fig. 2.6 to enable the boards enclosing the beam sides to be secured. Fig. 2.6 also shows the fire-resistances that can be achieved in constructions using this material.

2.5.2.4 Supalux board encasement

Supalux board, previously described in Section 2.4.1, is too thin to be edge-screwed and is fixed around the members being upgraded by screwing to continuous steel angle forming a framework around the section. For top flanges of beams the angle framing is shot-fired either to the flange or the floor soffit as shown in Fig. 2.7. Unlike Vermiculux, the Supalux board edges do not have rebates and thus joints between different lengths of boards require the insertion of Supalux backing strips to which the ends of the board lengths being jointed are screwed (see Fig. 2.7). Fire-resistances of up to two hours can be obtained with Supalux constructions and the material can be finished as for Vermiculux. The fixing methods used for Supalux encasement rule out its application to circular-section columns.

2.5.2.5 Vicuclad board encasement

Vicuclad is a rigid monolithic board material produced from exfoliated vermiculite and inorganic binders. The board has a smooth surface and is oatmeal in colour. The boards, available in two grades – 900R (1000 × 610 × 18 to 40mm thick) and 1050R (1000 × 610 × 45 to 80mm thick) – are capable of upgrading the fire-resistance of steel columns and beams by up to four hours.

The boards are cut to size on site and fixed to the existing sections using either a non-combustible cement, Vicuclad noggings and edge-nailing, as shown in Fig. 2.7; or, the boards can be fixed by screwing to galvanised steel angle fixed around the existing sections. Vicuclad can be plastered, tiled, painted, papered (after applying a plaster skim) or finished with a proprietary decorative coating such as Artex.

2.5.3 Spray-applied coatings

The majority of spray-applied materials are sprayed directly onto the surfaces of the beams and columns being upgraded and they therefore follow the existing sections' profiles.

2.5.3.1 Sprayed Limpet Mineral Wool – GP Grade

This proprietary material, previously described in Section 2.4.1, is sprayed directly onto the cleaned surface of the section being upgraded in one continuous application until the desired thickness has been obtained. The thicknesses required for various periods of fire-resistance are given in Fig. 2.7. Sprayed Limpet Mineral Wool – GP Grade can also be used to provide a hollow casing by spraying the material onto expanded metal lathing which has been wrapped around the steel sections.

2.5.3.2 Mandolite CP2 sprayed vermiculite-cement

Mandolite CP2 is a pre-mixed material based on vermiculite and Portland cement to which water is added on site. After mixing, it is sprayed directly onto the sections being upgraded, which must be clean and free of any surface impurities that might prevent adhesion. The Mandolite is built up in a series of passes of one or more coats until the required thickness is obtained. After drying, Mandolite CP2 forms an off-white textured surface which, if required, may be finished with a top coat paint. Fig. 2.7 gives the fire-resistances that can be obtained using Mandolite CP2.

2.5.4 Intumescent coatings

Intumescent materials, which are applied in very thin layers, have unique fire-resisting properties and comprise formulations of resinous binders, pigments, blowing agents and fillers.

These ingredients are stable and unreactive in situ at ambient temperatures and do not degrade with time. However, at high temperatures, as in a building fire, the ingredients undergo a well-defined chemical reaction which produces an expanded three-dimensional 'meringue-like' char which has a volume many times that of the original thin-layered coating. The char has low thermal conductivity, giving it good insulating characteristics against the heat and damaging effects of a building fire. Nullifire S602 is a typical proprietary example and consists of an intumescent solvent-based basecoat and a decorative topseal coat, which is available in any of the full BS 4800 colour range. The basecoat provides the fire protection; and the topseal, in addition to providing a decorative surface, protects the basecoat from mechanical damage and gives a 'wipe clean' surface. Both the intumescent basecoat and the decorative topseal coat can be applied by brush, roller or spray. Prior to application of the intumescent basecoat, the existing sections being upgraded should be coated with a suitable primer.

One of the principal advantages of using intumescent materials for upgrading existing iron and steelwork is that they are extremely thin (only 1mm for one-hour fire-resistance), and they are therefore ideal where, for architectural reasons, the existing profiles of ornate sections need to be preserved.

Nullifire also produce S603, a superior spray-grade version of S602; S605 designed for external exposure; S606 for high fire-ratings; and S607, a water-borne intumescent coating.

Fig. 2.7 indicates the fire upgrading obtainable using Nullifire intumescent protection and Fig. 2.8 shows how the process of intumescence takes place.

2.6 Upgrading the fire-resistance of doors

Where an existing building is improved or undergoes a change of use, it is likely that some of the existing internal doors will need either to be replaced or upgraded to comply with the requirements of the Building Regulations. Typical locations where fire doors are required include:

- doors separating flats or maisonettes from spaces in common use
- doors penetrating protecting structures (i.e., fire-resisting enclosures to stairwells, lift shafts, etc.)
- doors penetrating compartment walls (i.e., fire-resisting walls used to subdivide a building into compartments in order to restrict fire spread).

Fire doors will usually need to have a fire-resistance of sixty minutes, thirty minutes or twenty minutes (measured against the criterion of 'Integrity', see Section 2.3) and most types of existing door constructions are capable of being upgraded to twenty minutes or half an hour with relative ease. However, upgrading an existing door to one-hour standard is more difficult, and often produces a rather cumbersome result. Where one-hour fire doors are required, therefore, it is usually preferable to replace the existing doors rather than to attempt to upgrade them.

The techniques used to upgrade the fire-rating of existing timber-panelled doors are relatively simple and inexpensive. Several proprietary fire-resisting board materials are available in various thicknesses, and these can be nailed or screwed to the existing door's surface to achieve the standard required. Supalux board, previously described in Section 2.4.1, is used for a number of fire-upgrading applications and its use in the upgrading of existing doors is illustrated in Fig. 2.9. After fixing to the existing door, all screw/nail holes are filled and the new Supalux surface is painted to complete the upgrading of the door. It will be seen from Fig. 2.9 that, in addition to treating the surface of the door, it is also necessary to insert intumescent strips along the edges in order to obtain the required fire-rating. In the event of fire, the intumescent strips expand and seal the gaps around the door's edge, preventing the passage of smoke and flames. A further aspect requiring attention is the existing doorstops which must be at least 12mm deep.

As an alternative to the above methods, panelled doors can be upgraded to twenty-minutes fire-resistance

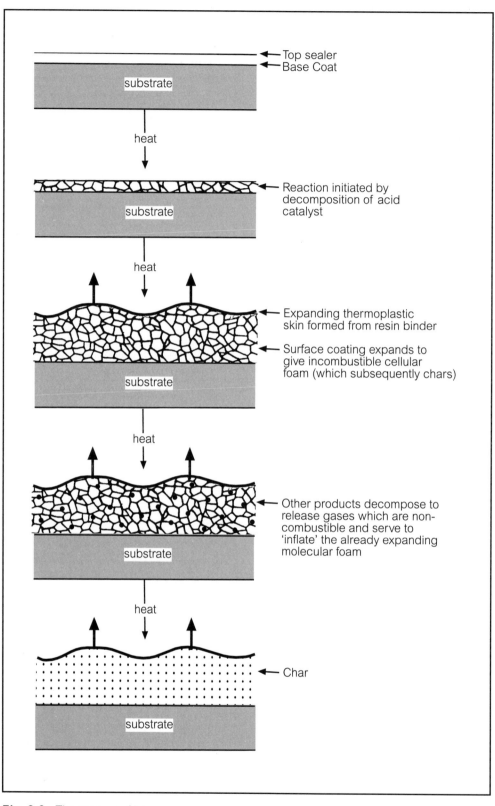

Fig. 2.8 The process of intumescence

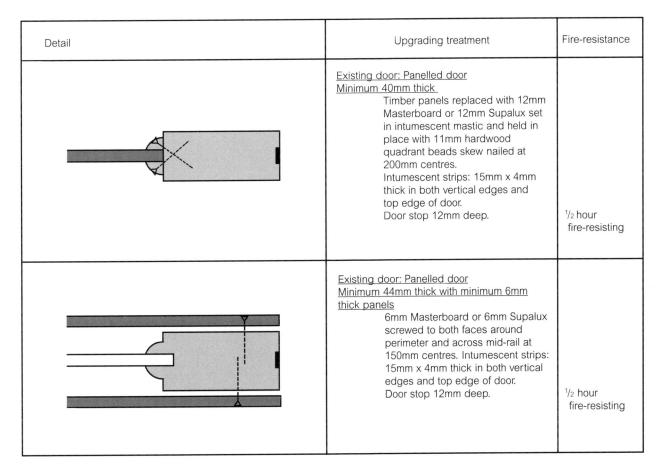

Detail	Upgrading treatment	Fire-resistance

	<u>Existing door: Panelled door</u>
	<u>Minimum 40mm thick</u>
	    Timber panels replaced with 12mm Masterboard or 12mm Supalux set in intumescent mastic and held in place with 11mm hardwood quadrant beads skew nailed at 200mm centres.
	    Intumescent strips: 15mm x 4mm thick in both vertical edges and top edge of door.
	    Door stop 12mm deep.
		½ hour fire-resisting

	<u>Existing door: Panelled door</u>
	<u>Minimum 44mm thick with minimum 6mm</u>
	<u>thick panels</u>
	    6mm Masterboard or 6mm Supalux screwed to both faces around perimeter and across mid-rail at 150mm centres. Intumescent strips: 15mm x 4mm thick in both vertical edges and top edge of door.
	    Door stop 12mm deep.
		½ hour fire-resisting

Fig. 2.9 Upgrading the fire-resistance of doors

using Nullifire System W intumescent basecoat and topseal (described in Section 2.4.1.4). However, for panelled doors to be upgraded to twenty-minutes fire-resistance they should have minimum thicknesses of solid timber as follows:

- all rails and stiles   35mm
- panels   8mm
- maximum gap door/frame   3mm

Intumescent strips along the door edges are also required as for the other upgrading methods described above.

2.7 Upgrading the fire-resistance of walls

In the majority of older buildings, the existing walls are normally masonry or brickwork, both of which have excellent fire-resistance and are, therefore, unlikely to need upgrading. For example, an unplastered 100mm thick brick wall will give a fire-resistance of two hours, which is more than adequate in virtually all circumstances. It is quite possible, however, that some of the internal walls within an existing building represent more recent additions which may be of less substantial construction, such as concrete blockwork or timber studding. Unplastered block walls 75mm and 100mm thick will give a fire-resistance of one hour and two hours respectively and are therefore, like brickwork and masonry, unlikely to need upgrading for fire-protection purposes. Many basic timber stud partitions, however, only give half-hour fire-resistance and therefore need upgrading if a higher standard is required. One of the simplest ways of upgrading such partitions is to nail an additional layer of 9.5mm plasterboard to each side, which will give a rating of one hour. If greater periods of fire-resistance are required, a wet plaster finish, using vermiculite-gypsum plaster if necessary, may be added, or thicker plasterboard used.

References

Building Research Establishment (1984) *Increasing the Fire-resistance of Existing Timber Floors* (Digest 208), 2nd edn, revised, BRE, Watford.

Department of the Environment (1992) *The Building Regulations 1991 Approved Document B: Fire Safety*, HMSO, London.

Department of the Environment, Transport and the Regions (1999) *Manual to the Building Regulations*, DETR, London.

Powell Smith, V. and Billington, M.J. (1999) *The Building Regulations Explained and Illustrated*, Blackwell Science, Oxford.

Stephenson, J. (1995) *Building Regulations Explained*, E. & F.N. Spon, London.

3
Upgrading internal surfaces

3.1 General

A highly effective means of improving the interior of an existing building as part of any refurbishment scheme, even in 'low-key' refurbishments, is to upgrade its internal surfaces. If the existing surfaces are in good condition, the necessary upgrading might only involve providing a new coat of paint, or wallcovering. On the other hand, in older buildings, and particularly those that have been neglected and/or disused for long periods, the existing surfaces may be in such poor condition that they need to be completely replaced. Where existing surfaces need to be upgraded, it will usually be the walls that involve most work, the upgrading of ceilings and floors tending to be less complicated.

3.2 Upgrading wall surfaces

In many buildings suitable for refurbishment, such as utilitarian factories, mills, warehouses, churches and agricultural barns, the structural walls may never have received any applied finishes. Such buildings, therefore, often consist of exposed masonry or brickwork which, in its present condition, is unlikely to be of adequate standard in any high-quality refurbishment scheme. Where plaster finishes have been applied they may have deteriorated beyond repair because of penetrating dampness or general neglect, especially where the building has been unoccupied, vandalised or open to the elements over a long period. In such cases, it will therefore be essential to upgrade the existing wall surfaces to satisfy modern standards and this can normally be achieved, after suitable preparation, either by applying a new plaster finish, or by applying some form of dry lining to the existing wall.

3.2.1 Plaster finishes

Provided the existing wall is not suffering from dampness and is in good condition, a normal plaster finish can be applied. Any existing surface finish should be removed and the brickwork or masonry joints well raked out to provide a suitable key for the new plaster. The wall should then be thoroughly brushed down to remove any dust, efflorescence salt or loose particles before applying the new finish. It is quite possible, particularly in older buildings, that the existing wall surfaces may be so uneven that a normal two-coat plaster finish will not be sufficient to give a true surface. In such cases, the application of two undercoats (a render and a floating coat) will usually be sufficient to fill out the deeper depressions. If this is not possible, then a dry-lining system may be the only solution.

Special plasters – specifically for replastering applications in refurbishment and upgrading work – have been developed, one such proprietary example being Thistle Renovating plaster. This is an undercoat plaster for general replastering applications which, with a final coat of Thistle Renovating Finish, provides a smooth, virtually inert, high-quality surface with earlier surface drying and a higher than normal resistance to efflorescence – often present in older buildings. Thistle Renovating plaster is a lightweight, retarded hemihydrate, pre-mixed gypsum undercoat plaster containing special aggregate and additives. The plaster has a controlled set which eliminates costly waiting time between coats and produces a finish that is free from shrinkage cracks. Where the wall to be replastered is damp, replastering should be delayed as long as possible to allow the background to dry out and any source of dampness must be identified and eliminated. Any salts brought to the surface of the background must also be carefully removed. Thistle Renovating plaster can be applied where only residual moisture is present, for example after most of the moisture in the wall has dried out following the insertion of a new damp-proof course or other remedial works to prevent laterally penetrating dampness. Low-suction backgrounds, such as engineering bricks or very dense masonry, should be treated prior to plastering with a neat coat of water-resisting bonding aid based on EVA or SBR latex which should be plastered over while still 'tacky'.

A proprietary plastering system specifically developed for application to walls following the installation of a new damp-proof course or remedial action to prevent penetrating dampness is Thistle Dri-Coat. This is a pre-mixed, lightweight cement-based undercoat plaster, incorporating expanded perlite aggregate and containing special additives which resist the passage of efflorescent and hygroscopic salts. When dry it also resists the passage of moisture but does not form a barrier to water vapour, therefore allowing any residual dampness to dry from the building structure. With a final coat of Thistle Board Finish or Thistle Multi-Finish, Thistle Dri-Coat provides a smooth, high-quality, virtually inert surface to walls containing residual dampness. It is essential, however, that the source of rising and/or penetrating dampness has been totally eliminated, and, ideally, the replastering should be delayed as long as possible. As with Thistle Renovating plaster, low-suction backgrounds, such as engineering bricks or very dense masonry, should be treated prior to plastering with a neat coat of water-resisting bonding aid based on EVA or SBR latex which should be plastered over while still 'tacky'.

3.2.2 Dry linings

Dry linings are a suitable and popular alternative to wet plaster as a means of upgrading wall surfaces in refurbishment work. If the existing wall is suffering from dampness, its source should be eliminated prior to applying the lining, since basic dry-lining systems are not suitable for use on damp backgrounds. It is possible,

however, with certain modifications, to use dry linings on damp backgrounds and this application is considered later. A further useful application for dry linings is in upgrading the thermal properties of external walls and this, also, is dealt with later.

Providing a dry-lining wall finish involves the fixing of gypsum plasterboard to the existing wall surface by one of a number of different techniques. Gyproc Wallboard, a plasterboard designed to receive direct decoration, is used, thereby eliminating the need for a wet skim coat of plaster. This gives the advantage of allowing the whole finishing process to be dry, involving no wet operations apart from jointing the board edges. Gyproc Wallboard is available in three standard thicknesses: 9.5, 12.5 and 15mm. Board widths are 900 or 1200mm and lengths range from 1800 to 3600mm. Where there is a risk of interstitial condensation following installation of the dry lining, Gyproc Duplex Wallboard should be used. This is a Gyproc Wallboard backed with a vapour-control membrane, available in three thicknesses: 9.5, 12.5 and 15mm. Board widths are 900 or 1200mm and lengths range from 1800 to 3000mm.

Three basic fixing techniques are used to install dry linings. Although a dry lining installed solely for the purpose of upgrading the quality of an internal surface finish would use only plain Wallboard, Figs. 3.1, 3.2, 3.3 and 3.4 show the use of thermal boards and other methods of incorporating insulation, as the fixing methods and detailing are similar for both.

3.2.2.1 Timber batten fixing

Timber battens, 50mm wide × 25mm thick, are fixed vertically to the existing wall at 400, 450 or 600mm centres, depending on the width of the boards used. It is likely that the existing wall surface will be uneven, and it is essential, therefore, that all depressions are packed out with timber or fibreboard pieces in order to achieve correct alignment of the battens. The boards are then nailed or screwed to the battens vertically, with 50mm × 25mm timber noggings inserted to support their horizontal edges. After the fixings and joints have been made good, the Wallboards may be decorated directly by painting, wallpapering or using any other suitable surface finish. Fig. 3.1 shows details of a timber batten dry-lining system.

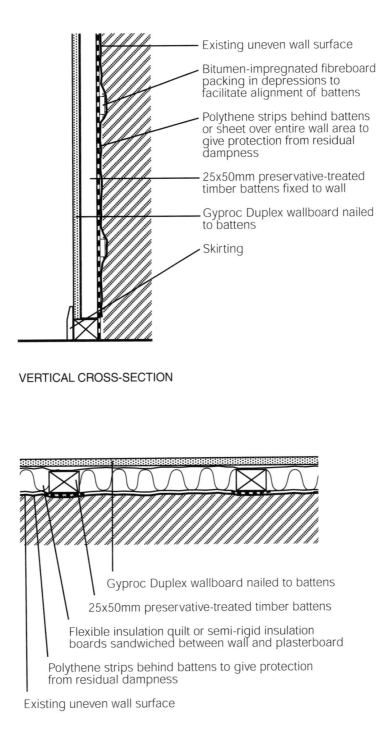

Existing uneven wall surface

Bitumen-impregnated fibreboard packing in depressions to facilitate alignment of battens

Polythene strips behind battens or sheet over entire wall area to give protection from residual dampness

25x50mm preservative-treated timber battens fixed to wall

Gyproc Duplex wallboard nailed to battens

Skirting

VERTICAL CROSS-SECTION

Gyproc Duplex wallboard nailed to battens

25x50mm preservative-treated timber battens

Flexible insulation quilt or semi-rigid insulation boards sandwiched between wall and plasterboard

Polythene strips behind battens to give protection from residual dampness

Existing uneven wall surface

HORIZONTAL CROSS-SECTION SHOWING THERMAL INSULATION

Fig. 3.1 Dry linings: timber batten fixing

3.2.2.2 Metal channel fixing

As an alternative to fixing the plasterboard dry lining to timber battens, metal furrings may be used. The Gyproc Dri-Wall MF system uses 50mm wide × 9.5mm deep zinc-coated mild-steel channels which are bonded vertically to the existing wall using special gypsum adhesive. Dabs of Gyproc Dri-Wall Adhesive, 200mm long, are applied to the wall at 600mm centres in vertical rows where each channel is to be fixed. The channels are then pressed on to the adhesive and aligned. Horizontal channels are fixed 30mm below the ceiling and 15mm above the finished floor level. The system is capable of accommodating irregularities in the background of up to 25mm, by using the adhesive to fill out any depressions that exist. When the adhesive has set, each 12.5mm Wallboard is screwed to its three vertical channels using a powered screwdriver. The fixings and joints are then made good and a suitable decorative finish applied to complete the upgrading of the wall. Where thermal laminates rather than plain Wallboards are used to provide the new internal surface, they are fixed to the

MF channels with a special gun-applied Gyproc Sealant as an adhesive, with screws as secondary fixings to the vertical board edges. Details of the Gyproc Dri-Wall MF system are shown in Fig. 3.2.

The Gyproc Gypliner Wall Lining system, similar in principle to the Dri-Wall MF system described above, uses lightweight metal track, channel and fixing brackets to form a framework for the fixing of plasterboards or thermal laminates. The framework is secured to the wall with metal brackets which are fixed to the wall, not by adhesive, but by Gypliner Anchors (pre-plugged nails). A major advantage of this system is that the metal fixing

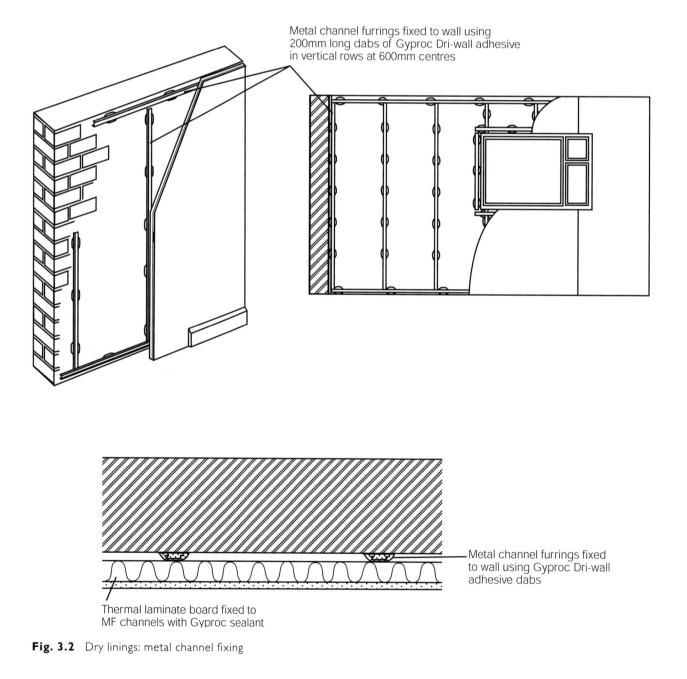

Metal channel furrings fixed to wall using 200mm long dabs of Gyproc Dri-wall adhesive in vertical rows at 600mm centres

Metal channel furrings fixed to wall using Gyproc Dri-wall adhesive dabs

Thermal laminate board fixed to MF channels with Gyproc sealant

Fig. 3.2   Dry linings: metal channel fixing

brackets allow a variable cavity depth behind the framework, of 25 to 130mm, to suit specific requirements such as the incorporation of services.

The system is installed by fixing metal track along the floor and ceiling to give the required stand-off (cavity), followed by anchoring of the metal fixing brackets to the wall. The vertical channels are then friction-fitted into the horizontal track and screwed to the fixing brackets. The new wall lining is completed by screwing Gyproc plasterboard or thermal laminate to the framing members.

3.2.2.3 Direct adhesive fixing

Plasterboard dry linings can be bonded direct to the existing wall surfaces using special adhesive, thereby ruling out the need to install timber battens or metal furrings. A widely used proprietary system is Gyproc Dri-Wall, which employs a special Gyproc Dri-Wall Adhesive to bond plain Wallboards or Gyproc Thermal Laminates direct to the existing wall surface. First, a continuous fillet of adhesive is applied to the existing wall perimeter, followed by dabs of adhesive applied in vertical rows 400, 450 or 600mm apart, depending on board width, with intermediate horizontal dabs at ceiling level. The board is offered up to the wall with the lower edge resting on packing strips and a footlifter is used to lift the board tight to the ceiling. Where thermal laminates are used rather than plain Wallboards, nailable plugs are installed to provide secondary mechanical fixings. Fig. 3.3 shows details of the Gyproc Dri-Wall TL system using thermal laminate plasterboard to form the dry lining.

As an alternative to the Gyproc Dri-Wall system, the Dri-Wall RF system provides a method of fixing boards directly to solid walls, including plastered walls in refurbishment work, using blobs of Gyproc Sealant. The blobs of sealant are gun-applied to the wall surface in vertical rows, as shown in Fig. 3.4. The board is offered up to the wall and fixed in the same way as the Dri-Wall Adhesive system, described above, nailable plugs being used to provide secondary fixings where thermal laminates are used.

3.3 Upgrading ceiling surfaces

The upgrading of existing ceiling finishes is generally less complicated than upgrading walls. Provided the structure above is sound, any conventional ceiling finish can be applied. In older buildings with timber floor structures, this will usually involve removal of the existing ceiling and its replacement with a new plasterboard ceiling. A useful alternative, particularly in buildings with high ceilings and where new services installations need to be concealed, is to install a suspended ceiling system which can be very effective in reducing the room height and providing a generous services void above.

In certain buildings the upgrading of existing ceilings may be closely associated with other upgrading work. For example, upgrading the fire-resistance of timber floors usually involves treatment to the existing ceiling (see Section 2.4) and it can therefore be designed to satisfy both upgrading requirements in one single operation.

3.4 Upgrading floor surfaces

3.4.1 Resurfacing with timber

A very wide range of options is available for the upgrading of existing floors, and, provided the structure is sound, any suitable finish can be applied. In many older buildings, the existing floors may be uneven and the first operation will involve resurfacing the subfloor in order to provide a level base for the new finish. With timber floors, the simplest solution is to overlay the existing floorboards with hardboard, or, where the surface is very uneven, plywood. In order to achieve a level surface, it may be necessary first to sand down high points and pack out depressions before fixing the new sheeting. In extreme cases, where the existing boarding is so uneven that levelling with a new surface is impossible, or where decay has occurred, it will be necessary to remove the boarding completely and replace it with new material. Existing concrete floors are less likely to need upgrading, apart from their surface finishes. However, if necessary, timber grounds or metal fixings can be inserted to receive a new wood surface.

3.4.2 Rescreeding

Where an existing concrete floor surface has deteriorated, an alternative to providing a new timber surface is to rescreed it, or add a new screed where one did not previously exist. This will require an extensive

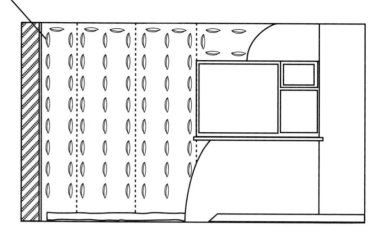

Dabs of Gyproc Dri-wall adhesive in vertical rows at 400, 450 or 600mm centres depending on board width

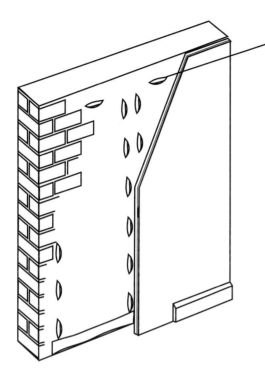

Combination masonry nail and plastic wall plug with expanding tip and countersunk head

Thermal laminate board fixed to wall using Gyproc Dri-wall adhesive dabs

Nailable plugs provide secondary mechanical fixing

Fig. 3.3 Dry linings: direct adhesive fixing

amount of preparation which may involve breaking up and removing an existing deteriorated screed and treating the exposed concrete surface to provide a suitable key for the new screed. It is also a time-consuming, labour-intensive task, and it may, therefore, be worth considering applying one of the proprietary floor-levelling compounds of the type described below.

3.4.3 Proprietary floor-levelling compounds

A widely used alternative to the above methods, where an existing floor surface is in poor condition and needs upgrading, is to apply a proprietary synthetic resin-based floor-levelling compound. Evo-Stik Floor Level and Fill is

a ready-mixed filler and self-levelling compound for preparing old or uneven floors prior to laying new coverings. It can be used over concrete, cement/sand screeds, ceramic tiles and asphalt. The material sets to an extremely durable, smooth surface which prevents the unsightly appearance and possible damage caused to the new floorcovering by any irregularities in the existing floor. Existing uneven floors are treated in three stages, as follows.

3.4.3.1 Preparation

Any loose or damaged areas in the floor should be chased out and dirt and grit brushed out from holes or cracks. The floor should then be thoroughly cleaned. The whole

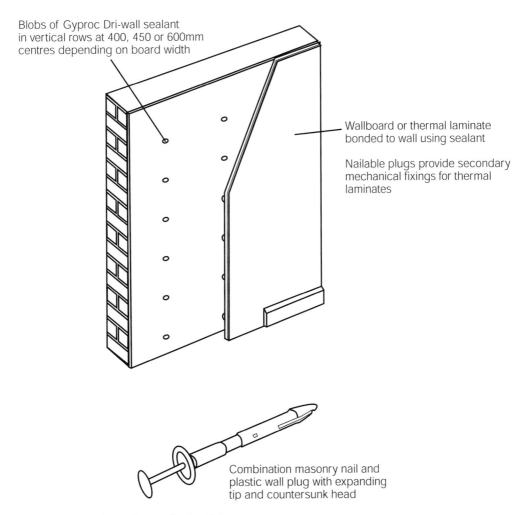

Blobs of Gyproc Dri-wall sealant in vertical rows at 400, 450 or 600mm centres depending on board width

Wallboard or thermal laminate bonded to wall using sealant

Nailable plugs provide secondary mechanical fixings for thermal laminates

Combination masonry nail and plastic wall plug with expanding tip and countersunk head

Fig. 3.4 Dry linings: direct adhesive fixing

floor must be sound and not subject to rising damp or any other structural defect.

3.4.3.2 Filling

The paste-like compound is applied with a trowel directly from its container in layers up to 20mm thick to fill any depressions in the floor surface. Each layer must be allowed to dry before the next is applied. The surface is then smoothed with a float, a perfect surface not being necessary if it is intended to level over the top.

3.4.3.3 Levelling

Any holes deeper than 3mm should be filled as previously described. The level-and-fill compound, which is diluted with water for the levelling operation to improve its flow capabilities, is poured on to the floor and spread evenly with a float to give a continuous layer 1mm thick, and no more than 3mm at any point. The self-levelling properties allow trowel marks to flow out.

A thin coat will take light foot traffic after drying overnight with good ventilation, and the new floorcovering can be laid after 24 hours.

References

Building Research Establishment (1998) *Replacing Plasterwork* (Good Repair Guide 18), BRE, Watford.

4
Upgrading the thermal performance of existing elements

4.1 General

An extremely important consideration, both in new construction and refurbishment work, is the provision of good thermal insulation to the external envelope in order to minimise heat loss, reduce heating costs, conserve fuel resources, reduce environmental pollution and maximise thermal comfort. Since the 1970s, the importance of providing adequate thermal insulation has been reflected by several changes to the Building Regulations, which now demand considerably greater standards of thermal insulation than were required earlier. It is therefore likely that most buildings which undergo refurbishment today will not, as they stand, comply with current Building Regulations regarding thermal insulation.

The construction of many older buildings is not conducive to the retention of heat within their interior spaces. In buildings with thick masonry external walls, heat is absorbed into the walls and therefore lost, satisfactory heating being difficult to achieve, particularly where intermittent heating cycles are operated.

In buildings with thinner, solid masonry or brick walls, heat loss through the structure can be considerable and some form of thermal upgrading will be necessary if heating costs are to be kept within reasonable limits. It should also be noted that untreated cavity walls do not reach the thermal standards required by current Building Regulations and thus thermal upgrading of cavity walls is often included in the refurbishment of more recently constructed buildings.

In addition to upgrading the external walls, it will be prudent also to attend to the existing roof which in most cases will not be insulated to current standards, and in some cases not insulated at all. A wide range of thermal upgrading techniques can be applied to existing roofs, the methods used depending principally on the nature of the existing roof structure.

4.2 Statutory requirements

Refurbishment schemes are required to comply with specified parts of the Building Regulations, including Part L ('Conservation of Fuel and Power', which includes thermal insulation requirements), if the works fall within the definition of a 'Material Change of Use'. The 'Material Change of Use' of existing buildings is defined and brought within the scope of the Building Regulations by Regulation 5, which gives its definition, and Regulation 6, which specifies the relevant requirements. Regulation 5 gives six cases defining 'Material Change of Use':

- when the building is used as a dwelling, where previously it was not
- when the building contains a flat, where previously it did not
- when the building is used as a hotel or boarding house, where previously it was not
- when the building is used as an institution, where previously it was not
- when the building is a public building, where previously it was not
- where a building is not exempt from control, where previously it was exempt under Schedule 2 of the Regulations

Typical examples of material changes of use would therefore include the refurbishment and conversion of:

- a redundant church into flats
- a riverside warehouse into a hotel
- a disused agricultural barn or stable into a house
- a redundant railway engine shed into a community centre.

Where a material change of use occurs under any of the six cases defined above, the following guidance is given by *Approved Document L: Conservation of Fuel and Power* on the necessity to upgrade the building's thermal performance:

- If the roof structure is being substantially replaced, thermal insulation should be provided to the standard required for new buildings.
- Where the roof is not being replaced, additional insulation should be provided to achieve a 'U'-value not exceeding 0.35 W/m^{2}K where the existing insulation provides a 'U'-value worse than 0.45 W/m^{2}K.
- If the ground-floor structure is being substantially replaced, thermal insulation should be provided to the standard required for new buildings.
- When substantially replacing complete external walls, or where the internal surfaces of external walls are being renovated over a substantial area, their thermal insulation should be upgraded by providing a reasonable thickness of insulation. If this is achieved using a dry-lining system the gaps between the lining and masonry should be sealed at the edges of window and door openings and at wall, floor and ceiling junctions to prevent infiltration of cold outside air.
- Where replacement windows are installed as part of the refurbishment they should be draught-stripped and have an average 'U'-value not exceeding 3.3 W/m^{2}K. However, it is recognised that this may be inappropriate in conservation work and in other situations where existing window design needs to be preserved.

It can be seen, therefore, that many refurbishment schemes will require thermal upgrading in order to comply with the Building Regulations and, even where it is not a statutory requirement, thermal upgrading will be a highly desirable feature of any refurbishment scheme because of the many benefits that it can provide.

4.3   Upgrading the thermal performance of walls

As explained above, many categories of refurbishment will include the addition or upgrading of thermal insulation to the existing walls. This is usually applied by adding a layer of insulating material to either the inside face or the outside face, or, in the case of cavity walls, by injecting an insulating fill into the cavity. The current Building Regulations 'U'-value requirement for external walls is 0.45 W/m^{2}K and, whichever method of upgrading is used, the aim should be to achieve this level of insulation if the refurbishment is to be of a high standard. With solid-walled buildings, the choice between internally applied or externally applied insulation will depend on two main factors: first, whether the building is heated intermittently or continuously; and secondly, the thermal capacity of the walls. Internally applied insulation is effective where the building is heated intermittently, since it prevents heat being absorbed by and lost into the walls, thereby giving a more rapid warm-up period. However, the addition of internal insulation will cause the existing wall structure to be colder, increasing the risk of condensation on or within it. It is therefore vital that an efficient vapour barrier be provided on the warm side of the new insulation to minimise this risk (see Section 6.6.2.3).

Externally applied insulation is effective where the building has thick walls of high thermal capacity, and is heated continuously. Heat is absorbed into, and retained by, the walls and 'given back' to the interior, and the risk of condensation is minimised. Externally applied insulation is also effective with thinner walls of low thermal capacity, regardless of whether the heating is intermittent or continuous.

The relative merits and disadvantages of externally and internally applied thermal insulation are given in Table 4.1.

4.3.1   Internally applied insulation

The application of thermal insulation to the internal surfaces of external walls is often combined with the upgrading of their surface finishes, and one of the most convenient ways of achieving this is to incorporate a layer of thermal insulation into a dry-lining system as follows.

Table 4.1   The relative merits and disadvantages of externally and internally applied insulation

Externally applied insulation	Internally applied insulation
1 Existing wall is kept warm and dry, thus increasing its insulation value and heat storage capacity	1 Application is not affected by weather
2 Cold bridging – where internal walls and floors abut the facade – is eliminated, therefore further reducing heat loss and surface condensation	2 Access to surfaces being treated is easier
	3 Has no effect on the external appearance of the building
3 The risk of interstitial condensation, within the thickness of the wall, is reduced	4 Cheaper than externally applied insulation
4 No internal work involved	5 Existing wall is not protected
5 Avoids disruption to, or masking of, existing interior wall finishes which may have to be preserved if the building is listed	6 Does not eliminate structural cold bridging
	7 Masks existing interior wall finishes
6 Less disruption to the occupants	8 Causes serious internal disruption
7 No loss of floor space	9 Eliminates surface condensation
8 Easier to apply around doors and windows	10 Perimeter floor space is reduced
9 Provides an improved external finish to buildings whose appearance has deteriorated because of weathering and atmospheric pollution	11 Difficult to apply around doors, windows and internal fittings
	12 Can be applied selectively to various parts of the building
10 Has a significant effect on the external appearance of the building and is therefore unsuitable for certain historic buildings where the existing appearance must be preserved	13 Can produce interstitial condensation risk
	14 Reduces heat protection of outside wall
	15 Practical limitations on thickness
11 More expensive than internally applied insulation	16 Reverse interstitial condensation risk with some insulants
12 Can be applied with almost no limit of thickness – will accommodate future standards	17 Fire risk with some insulants
13 Can correct adverse dew point situation	18 Produces similar savings in heat loss and energy consumption (up to 50%) to externally applied insulation
14 Produces similar savings in heat loss and energy consumption (up to 50%) to internally applied insulation	

4.3.1.1 Separate sandwich insulation

With basic timber batten dry-linings (see Section 3.2.2) a separate layer of insulation can be sandwiched into the space that has been created between the surface of the existing wall and the plasterboard as shown in Fig. 3.1. If standard-sized battens are used, the insulation thickness will be limited to 25mm, higher standards of insulation being obtained by using thicker battens to give a wider space, thereby enabling the insertion of a thicker layer of insulation. Suitable insulation materials include flexible quilts, or semi-rigid batts of glass mineral wool or rockwool.

Isowool Timber Frame Batts of glass mineral wool, 60mm thick, used in conjunction with a timber batten dry-lining system, will upgrade the 'U'-value of an existing 220mm solid plastered brick external wall from 2.17 to 0.52 W/m^2K. To achieve the Building Regulations standard of 0.45 W/m^2K, 80mm thick batts would be required.

Rockwool RW2 Flexible Insulating Slabs, 50mm thick, placed between the timber battens of a dry-lining system, will upgrade a 220mm solid plastered brick wall to 0.54 W/m^2K, and 75mm slabs will upgrade the same wall to 0.41 W/m^2K. The RW2 slabs are available in a range of thicknesses from 30 to 100mm.

4.3.1.2 Linings with pre-bonded insulation

The modern alternative to incorporating sandwich insulation is to apply a dry-lining comprising plasterboard with a layer of rigid insulation pre-bonded to it. Four proprietary examples are described below.

Styroliner LK: Styroliner LK (see Fig. 4.1) comprises plasterboard, 9.5mm thick, factory-bonded to a backing of Styrofoam LK closed-cell extruded polystyrene. The product is available with a tapered-edged manilla-faced plasterboard for direct decoration or, alternatively, with square-edged grey-faced plasterboard for finishing with a skim coat of plaster.

The closed-cell structure of the Styrofoam prevents capillary absorption of moisture and, in addition to thermal insulation, Styroliner LK provides an effective moisture barrier and vapour-check. Styroliner LK boards are 1200mm wide × 2438mm long and are available in seven overall thicknesses, from 21.5mm to 55.5mm. Styroliner LK can be fixed directly to most common forms of wall construction, including plastered surfaces, masonry and brickwork, using a suitable proprietary adhesive, such as Ardurit X7, applied either to the wall itself, or to the reverse side of the boards. The adhesive is applied to form a continuous band around the board perimeter with a vertical central band of adhesive. The boards are pressed against the adhesive and tightly against the ceiling. Secondary fixings are recommended in the form of at least four Tapcon self-tapping masonry screws per board, or any other proprietary fixing system.

As an alternative to direct adhesive fixing, Styroliner boards can be fixed to timber battens, similar to the method described in Section 3.2.2. The boards are fixed to the battens using galvanised plasterboard nails or screws. This method is more suited to very uneven backgrounds, fibreboard packing being used to fill any depressions in order to ensure correct alignment of the battens. The 'U'-value of an existing 220mm thick solid plastered brick external wall can be upgraded from 2.17 to 0.65 W/m²K by adding a 34.5mm Styroliner dry lining fixed with adhesive. To achieve the Building Regulations standard of 0.45 W/m²K, 55.5mm boards would be required. If timber batten fixing is used, the resulting 'U'-value will be improved further thanks to the cavity formed by the battens.

Gyproc Thermal Board: Gyproc Thermal Board (see Figs. 3.2, 3.3 and 3.4) is similar in principle to Styroliner. It comprises 9.5mm thick Gyproc Wallboard factory-bonded to a backing of expanded polystyrene insulating board. Gyproc Thermal Board is also available in a vapour-check grade for the control of interstitial condensation. The boards are available in lengths of 2700 and 2400mm × 1200mm wide and four overall thicknesses of 22, 30, 40 and 50mm. They should not be used to isolate dampness and are not suitable for use in continuously damp or humid conditions. In refurbishment projects where damp or rain penetration problems may exist, normal corrective measures, such as a new damp-proof course, tanking or external wall coating, should be taken prior to installation. The boards can be fixed to the existing wall by nailing to timber battens, screwing to metal channels, or with adhesive.

Timber-batten fixing of Gyproc Thermal Board is the same as for plain wallboard – described in Section 3.2.2 and illustrated in Fig. 3.1 – using plasterboard nails of the appropriate length. This method is the most suitable for very uneven backgrounds, since fairly deep depressions can easily be packed out with fibreboard to achieve alignment of the battens. The metal channel and adhesive systems, however, can also be used on uneven walls, provided the unevenness is not too excessive. For metal channel fixing of Gyproc Thermal Board, the Gyproc Dri-Wall MF system or the Gypliner Wall Lining system (previously described in Section 3.2.2.2 and illustrated in Fig. 3.2) are used. For adhesive fixing, either the Gyproc Dri-Wall TL system or the Gyproc Dri-Wall RF system is used. Both systems, described fully in Section 3.2.2 and illustrated in Figs. 3.3 and 3.4, also employ nailable plugs as secondary fixings. Gyproc Thermal Board is capable of significantly improving the thermal efficiency of existing walls. The 'U'-value of a solid 220mm thick plastered brick external wall can be upgraded from 2.17 to 0.62 W/m²K by applying 50mm Thermal Board fixed with adhesive.

Gyproc Thermal Board Plus: Gyproc Thermal Board Plus is composed of 9.5mm thick Gyproc Wallboard factory-bonded to a backing of closed-cell extruded polystyrene. With the exception of the insulant, the laminate is similar in all respects, including the methods of fixing, to Gyproc Thermal Board which uses expanded, rather than extruded, polystyrene as the insulating material. Board sizes are 2700 and 2400mm long × 1200mm wide and are available in five overall thicknesses of 27, 35, 42, 50 and 55mm. The thermal performance of closed-cell extruded polystyrene is superior to that of expanded polystyrene, and its inherent high resistance to the

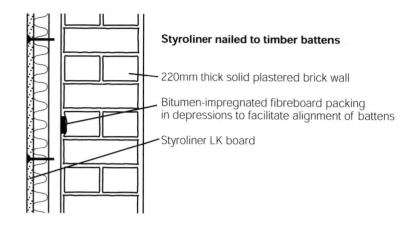

Styroliner nailed to timber battens

220mm thick solid plastered brick wall

Bitumen-impregnated fibreboard packing
in depressions to facilitate alignment of battens

Styroliner LK board

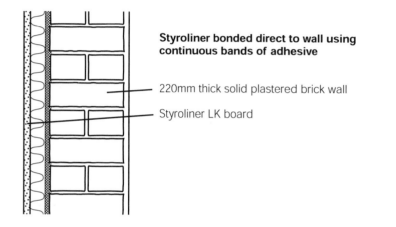

**Styroliner bonded direct to wall using
continuous bands of adhesive**

220mm thick solid plastered brick wall

Styroliner LK board

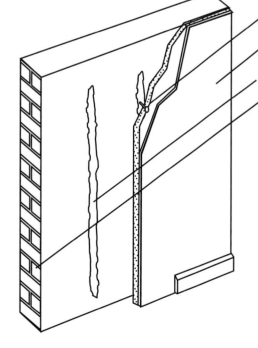

Tapcon self tapping masonry screws or similar
(minimum four per board)

Styroliner LK board

Perimeter and centre band of Ardurit x7 adhesive

220mm thick solid plastered brick wall

Fig. 4.1 Styroliner LK dry lining

passage of water vapour rules out the need for a separate vapour-check layer to be incorporated into the laminate where vapour resistance is required. The 'U'-value comparisons below illustrate the superiority of Thermal Board Plus over standard Thermal Board.

Gyproc Thermal Board Super. Gyproc Thermal Board Super is similar in all respects, including fixing methods, to the Gyproc thermal laminates described above, with the exception of its insulant, CFC-free phenolic foam, which is superior to both expanded and extruded polystyrene. The boards also incorporate an integral vapour-control layer as standard. The more efficient phenolic foam insulant enables high standards of insulation to be achieved by a relatively thin laminate with minimal encroachment on floor space. Board sizes are 2700 and 2400 long × 1200mm wide available in three overall thicknesses of 30, 40 and 50mm. Tables 4.2 and 4.3 illustrate the relative efficiencies of Gyproc Thermal Board, Thermal Board Plus and Thermal Board Super in upgrading an existing solid 220mm thick plastered external brick wall, 'U'-value 2.17 W/m^{2}K.

4.3.2   Externally applied insulation

Two of the most important factors that can determine whether externally applied insulation is used in preference to internally applied insulation are the condition and appearance of the existing external wall surfaces. For example, if the walls are constructed from fine, ornate masonry and they possess architectural and aesthetic merit, then masking them with externally applied insulation will not be appropriate. On the other hand, if the walls are uninteresting, in poor condition, or affected by dampness, then externally applied insulation may be the ideal solution, since, in one operation, their thermal performance, appearance and weather protection can be significantly improved. A number of other factors must also be considered before deciding whether or not to opt for external insulation, and these have been listed in Table 4.1.

Although the use of externally applied insulation systems rules out the need to disrupt the interior of the building, certain modifications to the exterior will be necessary to allow for the increase in the thickness of the wall. This may involve the extension of window sills, removal and repositioning of rainwater and waste pipes, provision of metal flashings, the accommodation of air bricks and other work to facilitate addition of the new insulation layer.

Four basic forms of externally applied thermal insulation are described here.

4.3.2.1   Thermal insulation behind conventional claddings

Where the existing wall has a tile or weatherboard external cladding, it may be possible to insert a layer of

Table 4.2   New 'U'-values of solid 220mm thick plastered brick external wall (existing 'U'-value 2.17 W/m^{2}K) after upgrading with Gyproc thermal laminates, overall thickness 50mm, fixed by adhesive

Type of thermal laminate	Thickness	New 'U'-value (W/m^{2}K)
Thermal Board	50mm	0.62
Thermal Board Plus	50mm	0.49
Thermal Board Super	50mm	0.36

Table 4.3   New 'U'-values of solid 220mm thick plastered brick external wall (existing 'U'-value 2.17 W/m^{2}K) after upgrading with Gyproc thermal laminates of various overall thicknesses, fixed by adhesive

Type of thermal laminate	Thickness	New 'U'-value (W/m^{2}K)
Thermal Board	50mm	0.62
Thermal Board Plus	55mm	0.45
Thermal Board Super	40mm	0.45

rigid or flexible insulation behind it. This will involve removal and replacement of the cladding, but has the advantage of maintaining the original exterior appearance of the building. It should be noted that, where this method is employed, provision should be made for adequate ventilation behind the cladding.

4.3.2.2 Expanded polystyrene boards with render finish

The Expolath Polystyrene external wall insulation system, for example (see Fig. 4.2), comprises 1220mm × 610mm stipple-coated expanded polystyrene insulation, with a density of 15kg/m^3, applied to the existing external wall surface and overlaid with expanded metal lathing to act as a key for the render finish. The insulation boards and lathing are secured mechanically to the wall using polypropylene, nylon or stainless steel fixing pins, which are tapped home into holes drilled through the lathing and insulation and into the existing brickwork or masonry. The render consists of an undercoat, topcoat and finish, the first comprising ordinary Portland cement, sand and a dry plasticiser/waterproofer with dry polymers which are factory-batched, needing only the addition of clean water on site. The factory-batched topcoat, either traditional or with polymer additives, is finished with decorative pre-washed and graded aggregates, or a range of acrylic decorative textured finishes. The insulation board is available in a range of thicknesses from 15mm to 100mm. An Expolath Polystyrene externally applied system, using 50mm thick insulation, will upgrade the 'U'-value of a 220mm solid plastered brick external wall from 2.17 to 0.50 W/m^{2}K. To achieve the Building Regulations standard of 0.45 W/m^{2}K, 60mm boards would be required.

As an alternative, the Terratherm PSB and PSM external wall insulation system (see Fig. 4.3) comprises 1000mm × 600mm expanded polystyrene boards fixed to the existing wall surface using adhesive, or a mechanically fixed rail system respectively. Two coats of basecoat mortar are then applied to the insulation, each with glass-fibre reinforcing mesh embedded into it. The adhesive and basecoat mortar consist of cement mixed with Terratherm Basecoat in the proportions 1:2.5 and 1:3 respectively. A primer is applied by roller to the final basecoat and the insulation system finished with either a coloured textured finish, 2mm thick, or a coloured fine aggregate finish 3mm thick applied by trowel. Additional

mechanical support, in the form of stainless steel and polypropylene fixings, supplements the adhesive in securing the expanded polystyrene boards to the existing wall.

The insulation boards are available in a range of thicknesses up to 100mm, the 80mm board upgrading a plastered 220mm thick solid brick wall from 2.17 to 0.39 W/m^{2}K.

4.3.2.3 Mineral wool slabs with render finish

The Rockwool RockShield rigid slab external wall insulation system (see Fig. 4.4) comprises mineral wool slabs, 900mm × 600mm, fixed to the existing wall surface using a combination of adhesive and mechanical fixings. The slabs receive an 8mm or 12mm thick render incorporating a reinforcing mesh to strengthen the system. The thicker render finish offers a higher tolerance to uneven wall surfaces. The render receives either Silcoplast ready-mixed finish, available in a stippled texture, or Liteplast finish, available in either stippled or dragged texture. Liteplast is supplied as a dry mortar requiring the addition of clean water on site. Both topcoat finishes are supplied in a wide range of colours. RockShield rigid slabs are available in thicknesses from 30mm to 100mm in 10mm increments: 30mm slabs will upgrade the 'U'-value of a 220mm solid plastered brick external wall from 2.17 to 0.69 W/m^{2}K; 60mm slabs will upgrade the same wall to 0.44 W/m^{2}K.

As an alternative to RockShield rigid slabs, RockShield facade lamellas, 1000mm × 200mm × 30 to 150mm thick, manufactured from the same material and fixed with adhesive only, may be used.

4.3.2.4 Closed-cell phenolic foam boards with render finish

The Thermalath reinforced external wall insulation system (see Fig. 4.5) comprises 2360mm × 600mm closed-cell phenolic foam insulation boards incorporating a factory-applied welded mesh render carrier, forming a system panel. The render carrier is formed from either a 1.6mm diameter galvanised, or a 1.5mm diameter stainless steel, wire mesh interwoven with a perforated layer of chipboard paper designed to provide uniform suction for the render. The system panels are mechanically secured to the external surface of the wall using stainless steel and polypropylene fixing pins which are

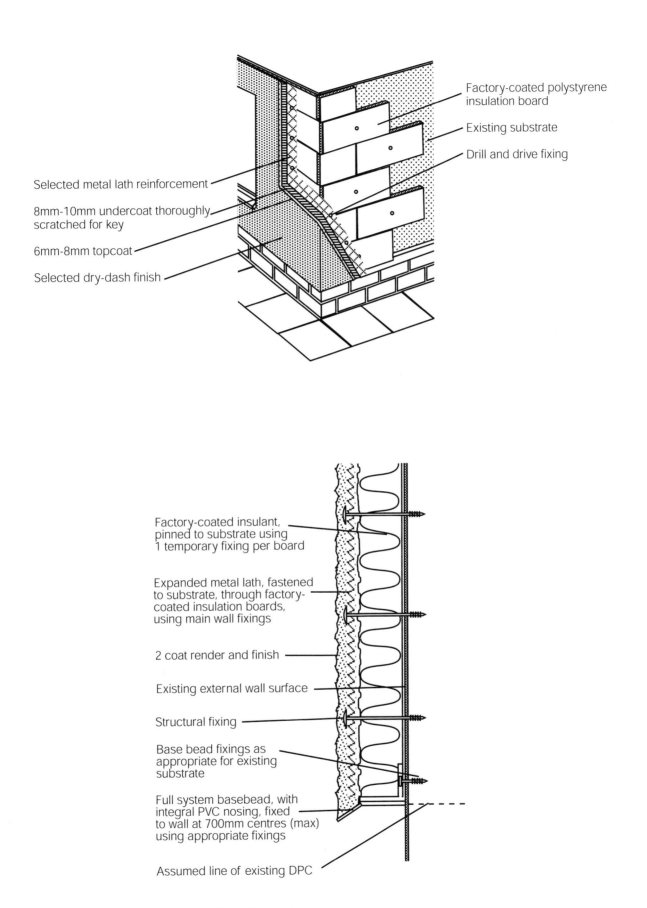

Factory-coated polystyrene insulation board

Existing substrate

Drill and drive fixing

Selected metal lath reinforcement

8mm-10mm undercoat thoroughly scratched for key

6mm-8mm topcoat

Selected dry-dash finish

Factory-coated insulant, pinned to substrate using 1 temporary fixing per board

Expanded metal lath, fastened to substrate, through factory-coated insulation boards, using main wall fixings

2 coat render and finish

Existing external wall surface

Structural fixing

Base bead fixings as appropriate for existing substrate

Full system basebead, with integral PVC nosing, fixed to wall at 700mm centres (max) using appropriate fixings

Assumed line of existing DPC

Fig. 4.2 Expolath Polystyrene externally applied insulation

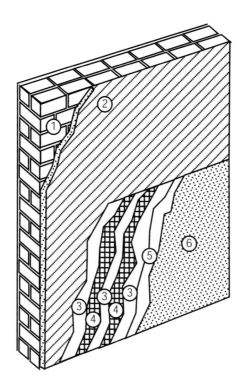

1. Existing wall surface
2. Expanded polystyrene board fixed with adhesive
3. Terratherm basecoat
4. Glass-fibre reinforcing embedded in basecoat
5. Primer applied by roller
6. 2mm thick textured or 3mm thick fine aggregate finish applied by trowel

Fig. 4.3   Terratherm PSB externally applied insulation

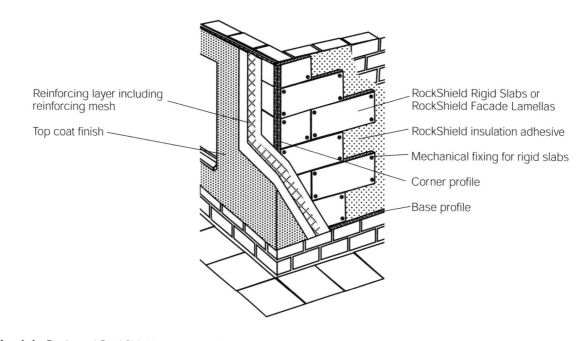

Reinforcing layer including reinforcing mesh

Top coat finish

RockShield Rigid Slabs or RockShield Facade Lamellas

RockShield insulation adhesive

Mechanical fixing for rigid slabs

Corner profile

Base profile

Fig. 4.4   Rockwool RockShield external wall insulation

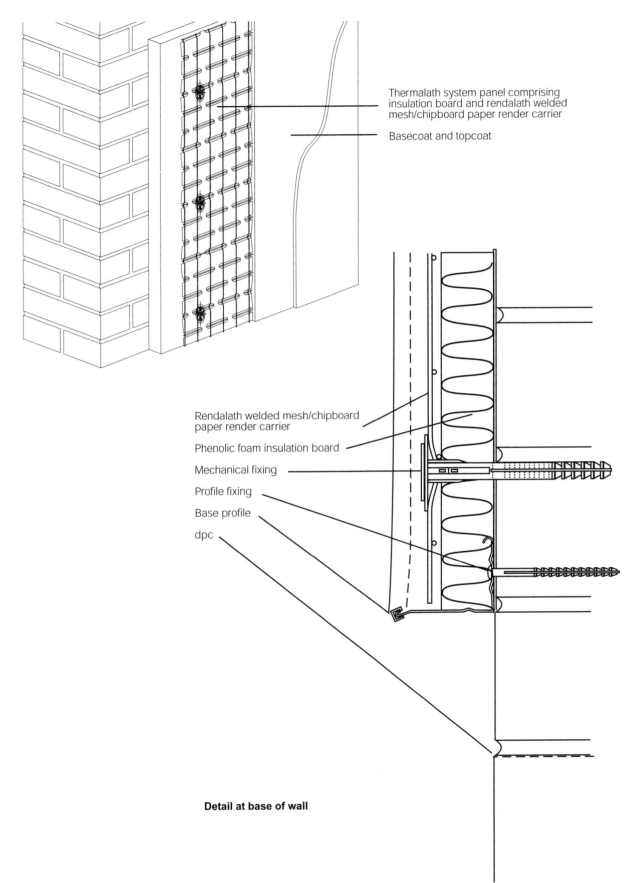

Thermalath system panel comprising insulation board and rendalath welded mesh/chipboard paper render carrier

Basecoat and topcoat

Rendalath welded mesh/chipboard paper render carrier

Phenolic foam insulation board

Mechanical fixing

Profile fixing

Base profile

dpc

Detail at base of wall

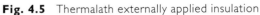

Fig. 4.5 Thermalath externally applied insulation

tapped into holes drilled through the panels and at least 50mm into the wall. The fixings are positioned at 300mm vertical centres and 600mm horizontal centres. The panels, once fixed to the wall, receive a 10–12mm thick cement-based standard or lightweight basecoat render. This is followed by one of a range of finishes including normal and lightweight cement-based dash receivers for dry spar dash and cement-based coloured Rencor Topcoat. The combined render basecoat and finishing coat thickness is 20mm in all cases.

The high-performance Thermalath phenolic foam insulation boards are supplied in a range of thicknesses between 25mm and 70mm. A Thermalath system using 25mm thick boards will upgrade the 'U'-value of a 220mm solid plastered brick external wall from 2.17 to 0.50 W/m²K. A 'U'-value of 0.44 W/m²K, which will meet current Building Regulations requirements, can be achieved using 30mm thick boards.

4.3.3 Injected cavity-fill insulation

This form of insulation was developed specifically for improving the thermal properties of existing cavity-walled buildings in order to reduce energy consumption and fuel costs. The insulation, which is injected into the cavity via holes drilled through the outer leaf, may be selected from a number of different proprietary materials. Injected cavity-fill materials currently in use include expanded polystyrene beads and mineral fibres, all of which are capable of greatly reducing the 'U'-value of a standard cavity wall.

Where a cavity-walled building requires thermal upgrading, this method is the most preferable solution, since it can be applied without affecting the existing exterior or interior surface, and with minimal disruption.

Rockwool EnergySaver cavity wall insulation (see Fig. 4.6) is a fully dry system which uses granulated Rockwool blown into an existing external wall cavity to a density of 30–50kg/m³ via holes drilled through the outer leaf. The holes are 18 or 25mm diameter at 1.5 metre centres in a staggered 'W'-pattern, normally located at mortar joint positions. Additional holes may be required, for example at window sills, at the tops of walls, around airbricks or under gables.

Rockwool EnergySaver blown mineral wool injected into the 50mm cavity of a standard brick outer-leaf/plastered dense blockwork inner-leaf cavity wall will

Fig. 4.6 Rockwool EnergySaver cavity wall insulation

improve the 'U'-value from 1.41 W/m²K to 0.55 W/m²K. If the wall has a 65mm cavity, the improved 'U'-value will be 0.45 W/m²K.

4.4 Upgrading the thermal performance of roofs

Loss of heat through the roof can represent up to a quarter of a building's total heat loss and thus thermal upgrading of the existing roof structure will be essential if future heating costs are to be minimised. Several techniques are available for use in upgrading roofs and the work can usually be carried out with the minimum of disruption to the building and its occupants.

The current Building Regulations 'U'-value requirement for pitched roofs is 0.25 W/m²K, and for flat roofs is 0.35 W/m²K (residential buildings) or 0.45 W/m²K (other buildings). Whichever upgrading method is used, the aim should be to achieve these levels of insulation in any high-standard refurbishment scheme.

4.4.1 Thermal upgrading of pitched roofs

Pitched roofs may be upgraded by inserting an additional insulating layer either at ceiling level, or at rafter level, immediately below the roof covering. Where a ceiling exists beneath the roof space, and provided the roof space is not intended for use, the insulation can be inserted at ceiling level to reduce heat loss into the void above, and ultimately to the exterior (see Fig. 4.7(a)). If,

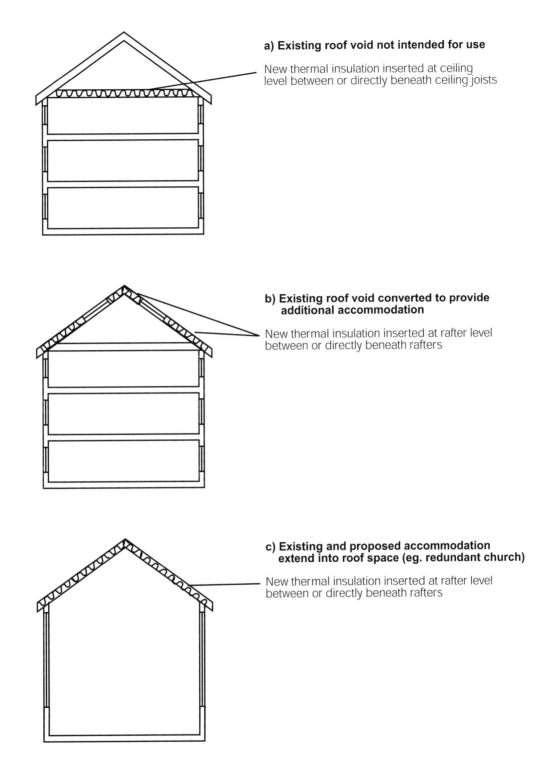

a) Existing roof void not intended for use

New thermal insulation inserted at ceiling
level between or directly beneath ceiling joists

**b) Existing roof void converted to provide
additional accommodation**

New thermal insulation inserted at rafter level
between or directly beneath rafters

**c) Existing and proposed accommodation
extend into roof space (eg. redundant church)**

New thermal insulation inserted at rafter level
between or directly beneath rafters

Fig. 4.7   Upgrading the thermal performance of pitched roofs

however, the roof space is to be converted into
accommodation in the refurbishment/alteration scheme,
it will be necessary to provide the new insulation at rafter
level (see Fig. 4.7(b)). The new insulation may also have
to be inserted at rafter level in buildings where no ceiling
exists and where the accommodation extends into the

roof space. Typical examples of this include redundant
churches and agricultural barns, where the existing open
roof space is retained to preserve the original character;
and old factories and warehouses, where ceilings were
not normally provided beneath the roof space (see Fig.
4.7(c)).

The various methods that can be used to upgrade the thermal performance of pitched roofs are described below and illustrated in Fig. 4.8.

4.4.1.1 Insulation mats at ceiling level

Where a ceiling exists beneath the roof space, the simplest and most common solution is to lay the new insulation immediately above the ceiling, between the joists or the lower ties of the roof trusses. Flexible insulation mats, supplied in rolls of varying widths and thicknesses, are a cheap and efficient way of upgrading thermal insulation using this method (see Fig. 4.8(a)).

When insulation is provided directly above the existing ceiling in this way, it is essential to ensure that the roof space above the insulation is properly ventilated. Providing better insulation at ceiling level has the effect of reducing the temperature within the roof space which, in turn, increases the risk of condensation. Effective cross-ventilation is therefore essential in order to minimise the condensation risk and avoid potential damage to the roof structure. This can be achieved by forming ventilation openings at the eaves and inserting air-bricks in gable ends.

Rockwool Rollbatts are lightweight Rockwool insulation mats available in thicknesses of 80, 100 or 150mm × 400, 600 or 1200mm wide × up to 5 metres long depending on thickness, supplied in rolls. Thicknesses greater than 150mm are obtained by using double layers of Rollbatt.

The 'U'-value of an existing uninsulated, tiled 30° pitch roof with sarking felt and a plasterboard ceiling with 38 × 97mm joists at 600mm centres can be improved from 2.0 W/m²K to 0.27 W/m²K using 150mm thick Rockwool Rollbatts. A total Rockwool Rollbatt thickness of 180mm (100mm + 80mm) will achieve a 'U'-value of 0.19 W/m²K.

4.4.1.2 Loose-fill materials at ceiling level

As an alternative to laying insulating quilts above the existing ceiling, loose-fill insulating materials may be used. These include blown mineral wool, expanded vermiculite and expanded polystyrene beads, all of which can be inserted in varying thicknesses according to the degree of thermal upgrading required (see Fig. 4.8(b)). One disadvantage of using these materials is that their loose, lightweight nature can cause problems such as leakage

via ventilation openings and inadvertent blocking of services ducts, flues, and so on. As with insulating quilts, it will also be necessary to ventilate the roof space in order to minimise the risk of condensation (see Section 4.4.1.1 above).

Rockwool EnergySaver blown loft insulation comprises granulated Rockwool blown through a delivery hose directly between and over the existing ceiling joists to the required thickness. The 'U'-value of an existing uninsulated, tiled 30° pitch roof with sarking felt and a plasterboard ceiling with 38 × 97mm joists at 600mm centres can be improved from 2.0 W/m²K to 0.22 W/m²K using a 175mm thickness of Rockwool Blown Loft Insulation.

4.4.1.3 Thermal boards at ceiling level

Where the existing ceiling is in poor condition and is beyond economic repair, its replacement with a proprietary thermal board such as Gyproc Thermal Board or Styroliner (see Section 4.3.1) will be a viable solution (see Fig. 4.8(c)). In this way, a new plasterboard ceiling – capable of receiving direct decoration – and an additional insulating layer are provided in a single operation. A further advantage is that thermal boards can be obtained with an integral vapour barrier, sandwiched between the plasterboard and the factory-bonded insulation, therefore significantly reducing the risk of condensation in the roof space above.

4.4.1.4 Insulation mats or boards at rafter level

Thermal insulation must be provided at rafter level where the roof is to be converted into usable accommodation or where no ceiling exists and the upper rooms extend into the roof space. In most cases, a rigid internal lining of plasterboard or similar material will be fixed to the rafters and the insulation can therefore be sandwiched between the lining and the roof covering. The insulating material will need to be held in position to prevent settlement or slipping down the roof slope which could result in gaps opening between sections. This rules out the use of loose-fill materials, the most preferable being rigid insulation boards supported at regular intervals down the roof slope by cross-battens between the rafters. Suitable materials include insulation mats of glass-wool or rock-fibre and rigid boards of expanded polystyrene or polyurethane foam, all of which are

New thermal insulation at ceiling level

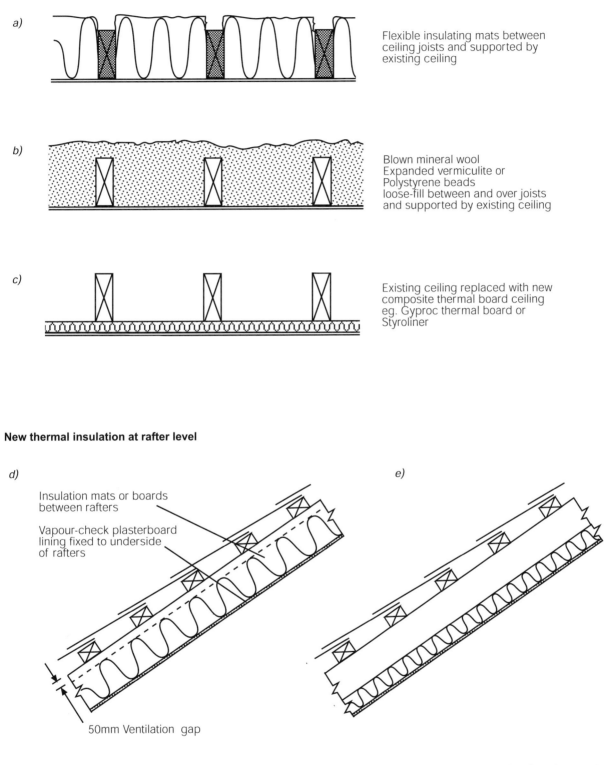

a) Flexible insulating mats between ceiling joists and supported by existing ceiling

b) Blown mineral wool
Expanded vermiculite or
Polystyrene beads
loose-fill between and over joists
and supported by existing ceiling

c) Existing ceiling replaced with new composite thermal board ceiling eg. Gyproc thermal board or Styroliner

New thermal insulation at rafter level

d)
Insulation mats or boards between rafters

Vapour-check plasterboard lining fixed to underside of rafters

50mm Ventilation gap

New plasterboard lining supporting separate insulation mats or boards inserted between rafters

e)
New composite thermal board lining (eg. Gyproc thermal boards or Styroliner) nailed to underside of rafters

Fig. 4.8 Upgrading the thermal performance of pitched roofs

available in a range of sizes and thicknesses to suit individual requirements.

Where this method is used it is essential that a ventilated airspace of at least 50mm is provided between the insulation and the sarking felt in order to minimise the risk of condensation. The condensation risk can also be reduced by using vapour-check plasterboard (see Fig. 4.8(d)). A suitable proprietary system of this type is Isowool General Purpose Roll glass-wool insulating mat, available in a range of thicknesses from 60 to 200mm and widths of up to 1200mm, with an internal lining of Gyproc Wallboard Duplex plasterboard. The 'U'-value of a typical uninsulated pitched roof covered with slates or tiles with a sarking felt underlay can be upgraded from 2.0 W/m^2K to 0.25W/m^2K using 150mm thick Isowool General Purpose Roll lined with Gyproc Wallboard Duplex. In order   to fit this thickness of insulation between the rafters and maintain a 50mm airspace, it will be necessary to increase the rafter depth by fixing additional battens to the face of the existing rafters.

A suitable alternative to using a plasterboard lining and separate sandwiched insulation is to use one of the proprietary thermal boards described earlier (see Section 4.4.1.3 above). Styroliner or Gyproc Thermal Board (see Section 4.3.1), fixed to the underside of the rafters, provide an internal lining, thermal insulation and a vapour check in one operation (see Fig. 4.8(e)).

The thermal upgrading achieved using this method can be improved further by the addition of Isowool General Purpose Roll above the thermal board and between the rafters. For example, 50mm Thermal Board Super, fixed to the undersides of the rafters and overlaid with 60mm thick Isowool General Purpose Roll, will upgrade the 'U'-value of a typical uninsulated pitched roof from 2.0 W/m^2K to 0.25 W/m^2K.

4.4.2   Thermal upgrading of flat roofs

The method used to upgrade an existing flat roof will depend to some extent on its construction. Concrete flat roofs can be upgraded only by adding the new insulation either beneath the slab at ceiling level or on top of the slab. With timber flat roofs, a third option is available, this being to insert the insulation within the void between the ceiling and the roof covering. It should, however, be borne in mind that, where possible, upgrading methods which produce a 'cold roof' should be avoided as this would involve providing adequate ventilation to remove moisture vapour. A number of methods to upgrade flat roofs are described next.

4.4.2.1   Thermal boards at ceiling level

The simplest and most cost-effective means of upgrading a flat roof is to provide thermal boards at ceiling level. Proprietary boards, such as Gyproc Thermal Board or Styroliner (see Section 4.4.1.3 above), can either be fixed directly beneath the existing ceiling or be used to replace the existing ceiling if it is in a poor state of repair. The use of thermal board for upgrading rules out the need to gain access to the void (in the case of timber roofs), does not involve external work, and provides a new ceiling capable of direct decoration. However, it does involve some internal disruption and inconvenience to occupants, and it may also be inappropriate where the existing ceiling has ornate plasterwork.

The provision of additional insulation on the underside of the roof structure in this way produces a 'cold roof', that is, the temperature of the roof structure is at or near that of the outside air. This condition significantly increases the risk of condensation within the roof construction and it is therefore essential that precautions are taken to reduce this risk. The use of thermal board with an integral vapour barrier sandwiched between the plasterboard and insulation will minimise the occurrence of condensation, and, if the roof is of timber, the void should also be ventilated.

4.4.2.2   Insulation mats or boards at ceiling level

This method is only applicable to timber flat roofs and involves inserting the new insulation in the void between the ceiling and roof covering. It is therefore appropriate only in cases where the existing ceiling is in poor condition and needs replacing, and involves inserting insulation mat or rigid insulation boards between the roof joists prior to fixing a new plasterboard ceiling. This method has the advantage of allowing a much thicker layer of insulation to be provided, since the void between the ceiling and roof covering will be at least 100mm. As with the previous method, however, a cold roof will result and it will therefore be necessary to use a vapour-check plasterboard and to ventilate the roof void.

4.4.2.3 Rigid insulation boards on top of existing roof structure

In some cases, it may be necessary to remove and replace the exterior roof covering if it has deteriorated beyond repair, and in this event, new, rigid insulation can be provided before laying the new covering. The Rockwool Hardrock range of insulation boards can be applied to existing timber, concrete and metal roofs to improve their thermal performance. Hardrock Standard Roofing Board sized 1200mm × 600mm is available in thicknesses from 30mm to 100mm, and the 'U'-value of an existing timber-joisted flat roof with plasterboard ceiling can be upgraded to 0.35 W/m²K using 90mm thick boards. A 'U'-value of 0.25 W/m²K can be achieved using a total thickness of 130mm Hardrock Standard Roofing Board (2 × 65mm boards).

Although providing the new insulation on top of the existing roof structure involves external work, there are a number of significant advantages:

- Adding the insulation externally produces a 'warm roof', which minimises the risk of condensation within the roof construction.
- There is no disruption to interior finishes and fittings.
- The occupants of the building undergo minimal inconvenience since no interior work is necessary.

4.4.2.4 Rigid insulation boards on top of the existing roof covering

If the existing roof covering is still waterproof and in good physical condition, the new thermal insulation can be added on top without having to take up the existing covering. In addition to the advantages of producing a 'warm roof', the lack of disruption to interior finishings and fittings, and minimal inconvenience to occupants, such systems, as they are laid on top of the existing waterproof covering, provide the latter with protection from frost action, high temperatures caused by solar radiation, and mechanical damage.

Roofmate SL is a proprietary closed-cell extruded polystyrene insulation board specifically developed for the external insulation of flat roofs. The closed-cell structure of Roofmate SL gives the boards a high resistance to moisture absorption, providing resistance to freeze/thaw cycles, and ensuring that the boards retain their insulation properties throughout the life of the building. The Roofmate SL insulation boards are 1250mm long × 600mm wide × 50, 60, 75, 90, 100 and 120mm thick with rebated (ship-lap) edges. Roofmate SL can be used to upgrade the thermal insulation of timber, concrete and metal roofs finished with built-up felt, asphalt and other waterproofing systems, the procedure being as follows:

- The existing roof surface is swept clean of any loose gravel chippings. Well-bonded gravel chippings need not be removed but should be covered with a loose-laid cushioning layer such as Ethafoam 222E extruded polyethylene foam sheet. The existing waterproof layer should be checked prior to laying the new insulation and any necessary repairs carried out as Roofmate SL is not a cure for membrane failure.
- The Roofmate SL insulation boards are laid loose in a brick-bond pattern with their rebated edges pushed tightly together.
- The insulation boards are covered with a ballast layer of either gravel (20–40mm nominal size), 50 to 90mm thick, or concrete paving slabs 40 or 50mm thick. The thickness of the loading-layer will depend upon the thickness of insulation boards selected.

While 90mm thick Roofmate SL insulation boards with a 75mm gravel loading-layer will improve the 'U'-value of an uninsulated 200mm thick flat concrete roof with a 50mm screed and plastered ceiling to 0.30 W/m²K, 120mm thick boards with 90mm of gravel will achieve 0.24 W/m²K.

An alternative to the above, produced by the same manufacturer, is Roofmate LG insulation board. This consists of Roofmate closed-cell extruded polystyrene insulation board, self-finished with a 10mm thick protective layer of modified mortar on the top surface. Because it avoids the need for overall ballasting, it is lighter than the Roofmate SL system being specifically designed for lightweight roofs that cannot support the weight of the ballast required for Roofmate SL.

The Roofmate LG boards are 1200mm × 600mm × 60, 70, 90, 110 or 130mm overall thickness and have a specially designed tongue-and-groove detail on their long sides to ensure that they interlock when laid: 90mm (overall) thick Roofmate LG insulation boards will improve the 'U'-value of an uninsulated timber-joisted roof with three layers of felt on 19mm woodwool slabs and a plasterboard ceiling from 1.7 W/m²K to 0.34 W/m²K; 130mm thick boards will achieve 0.24 W/m²K.

4.5   Upgrading the thermal performance of floors

Heat loss through the floor of a building is substantially less than that via the external walls and roof, and, for this reason, the floors are often ignored when refurbishing and upgrading buildings. However, as previously indicated in Section 4.2, current Building Regulations requirements will have to be met if a ground-floor structure is being substantially replaced. In any event, all energy-conscious refurbishment/improvement schemes should upgrade the thermal performance of ground and other exposed floors where possible. The current Building Regulations require all exposed floors and ground floors to have a 'U'-value of 0.45 W/m²K or less.

Styrofloor is a factory-bonded laminate of 18mm thick P5 chipboard and Styrofoam closed-cell extruded polystyrene insulation board 16, 20, 25, 35 or 50mm thick, giving overall thicknesses of 34, 38, 43, 53 and 68mm respectively. The boards are 2400mm long × 600mm wide with tongued and grooved edges to facilitate effective jointing. Styrofloor boards can be laid on existing concrete or timber ground floors to upgrade their thermal insulation and provide a new floor finish in a single operation. All skirtings and other fixtures should first be removed. Uneven floors can be levelled using a proprietary levelling compound; and if particularly damp conditions exist, and in the absence of a damp-proof membrane, 1000-gauge polythene sheeting should be laid under the Styrofloor. Prior to laying the boards, the floor should be cleaned and all loose material removed. The boards are laid with cross-joints staggered to produce a brick pattern and with a 10–12mm expansion gap at all wall abutments.

The boards are not secured to the floor but all of the tongued and grooved edge-joints are bonded with water-resistant PVA adhesive. A suitable compressible foam filler should be fitted around the perimeter of the floor between the boards and walls before the skirting boards are refixed.

Styrofloor boards are capable of upgrading the thermal insulation of existing concrete and timber ground floors to the current Building Regulations standard of 0.45 W/m²K or better.

(Note: Styroliner (Section 4.3.1) and Styrofloor (Section 4.5) are registered trademarks of Panel Systems Ltd.)

References

Building Research Establishment (1990) *Choosing between Cavity, Internal and External Wall Insulation* (Good Building Guide 5), BRE, Watford.

Building Research Establishment (1993) *Double Glazing for Heat and Sound Insulation* (Digest 379), BRE, Watford.

Building Research Establishment (1994) *Thermal Insulation – Avoiding Risks*, BRE, Watford.

Department of the Environment and The Welsh Office (1995) *The Building Regulations 1991 Approved Document L: Conservation of fuel and power*, HMSO, London.

Department of the Environment, Transport and the Regions (1999) *Manual to the Building Regulations*, DETR, London.

Powell Smith, V. and Billington, M.J. (1999) *The Building Regulations Explained and Illustrated*, Blackwell Science, Oxford.

Richardson, B.A. (1991) *Defects and Deterioration in Buildings*, E. & F.N. Spon, London.

Stephenson, J. (1995) *Building Regulations Explained*, E. & F.N. Spon, London.

5
Upgrading the acoustic performance of existing elements

5.1 General

It is now universally accepted that unwanted, intrusive sound is a common environmental problem, and one which can be alleviated to a large extent by paying special attention to the acoustic design and construction of buildings. It is also possible, by using a wide range of techniques, to improve considerably the acoustic performance and sound insulation of elements in existing buildings when refurbishment and alteration work are carried out.

5.2 Statutory requirements

Part E of the Building Regulations, 'Resistance to the Passage of Sound', applies only to dwellings, there being no statutory requirement to provide sound insulation in other types of building. Both new dwellings and buildings converted to dwellings must comply with the acoustic standards laid down in Part E of the Regulations. As stated in Section 4.2, conversion/refurbishment schemes are required to comply with specified parts of the Building Regulations if they undergo a 'Material Change of Use' – Section 4.2 defines the six Material Change of Use cases. With regard to the acoustic performance of buildings, the works must comply with Part E of the Building Regulations ('Resistance to the Passage of Sound') in the cases of the building being used as a dwelling where previously it was not; and containing a flat, where previously it did not.

Note that six Material Change of Use cases are specified in Building Regulation 5 (see Section 4.2), but compliance with Part E is enforced only in the two cases referred to above, that is conversion to dwellings and flats.

There are, however, many other examples where good sound insulation is important: in hotels, boarding houses, hostels, and so on, where sleeping accommodation is provided, and where intrusive noise is unacceptable to the occupants. Walls and floors separating offices from workshops in industrial buildings, or consulting rooms from waiting areas in medical centres, are further common examples illustrating the importance of good sound insulation. Despite the fact that the Building Regulations do not enforce acoustic requirements in such cases and the multitude of other situations where good sound insulation is desirable, it is essential that all high-quality refurbishment/conversion schemes incorporate acoustic upgrading where necessary to ensure satisfactory environmental conditions for their occupants. Designers are therefore advised to use Part E of the Building Regulations as a guide for all refurbishment/conversion schemes where sound insulation is a key factor.

In order to meet the sound-insulation requirements of Part E of the Building Regulations, conversions of buildings to dwellings or flats must comply with *either* section 5 of *Approved Document E: Resistance to the Passage of Sound* (which gives a number of acceptable upgrading constructions for walls and floors), *or* section 6 of *Approved Document E* (which permits the repetition of constructions that have been built and tested in a building or a laboratory).

It is possible that the existing wall and floor constructions already meet the requirements for sound insulation without the need for upgrading. This can be demonstrated by either showing that the existing wall or floor is generally similar to one of the acceptable constructions for new buildings, given in sections 1 and 2 of *Approved Document E* (for example, its mass is within 15% of the section 1 and 2 constructions), *or* carrying out a field test on the construction in accordance with the method specified in section 6 of *Approved Document E*.

It should be understood at this point that floors and walls may need to be resistant to the passage of one or both of the following types of sound:

- Airborne sound: airborne sources, such as speech, musical instruments and audio speakers, create vibrations in the surrounding air which spread out and, in turn, create vibrations in the enclosing walls and floors (elements). These vibrations spread throughout the elements and into connecting elements, forcing the air particles next to them to vibrate, and it is these new airborne vibrations that are heard as airborne sound.

- Impact sound: impact sources, such as footsteps, create vibrations directly in the element they strike. These vibrations then spread throughout the element and into connecting elements, forcing the air particles next to them to vibrate, these new vibrations being heard as impact sound.

5.3 Upgrading the acoustic performance of separating walls

Traditional brickwork or blockwork separating walls between semi-detached houses, terraced houses, flats and maisonettes will normally provide adequate sound insulation, thereby preventing noise nuisance between occupancies. However, some occupants may be less tolerant of noise, and some may generate unacceptably high levels of noise. Building Regulation E1 requires that any wall separating one dwelling from another dwelling or from another building, *or* any wall separating a habitable room in a dwelling from any other part of the same building which is not used exclusively with that dwelling, shall resist the transmission of airborne sound. Thus, in conversion/refurbishment work it will be necessary to ensure that such walls are constructed or upgraded to comply with the guidance contained in *Approved Document E* to the Regulations. The following methods are suitable where there is a need to upgrade

the acoustic performance of existing brickwork or blockwork separating walls.

5.3.1 Timber stud frame independent leaf

One of the most effective ways of upgrading the sound insulation of an existing separating wall is to add a separate leaf on one or both sides of the wall to provide a clear air gap, together with the inclusion of a sound-absorbent material in the cavity. This is the acceptable upgrading method given in section 5 of *Approved Document E* to the Regulations. If the existing masonry wall is at least 100mm thick and plastered on both faces, a separate leaf need only be provided on one side. For any other construction, separate leaves should be built on both sides. The new independent leaf construction (see Fig. 5.1) comprises two layers of 12.5mm thick Gyproc SoundBloc Wallboard plasterboard with staggered joints, fixed to a timber stud framework. It is essential that the studding is fixed only to the existing floor and ceiling, and not to the wall itself, since any contact with the wall will adversely affect the degree of sound reduction obtained. The best procedure is to fix the head and sole plates to the existing ceiling and floor respectively, and insert the vertical studs between them to give a continuous gap between the stud framing and the wall. Sound-absorbent mineral wool, 25mm thick, with a density of at least 10kg/m^2, is hung either between the vertical timber studs or against the existing wall face by means of a timber-fixing batten along the top edge. The independent leaf should be sealed around its perimeter with mastic or tape. Adequate spacing between the new independent leaf and the existing wall is of vital importance and *Approved Document E* requires a gap of at least 25mm between the inside face of the plasterboard and the existing wall face, and a gap of at least 13mm between the inside face of the studding and the wall face. Any other type of studding, such as proprietary metal studding, may be used as an alternative to timber.

A wider gap than the minimum required by *Approved Document E* will further improve the sound insulation upgrading, and the construction in Fig. 5.1 shows a clear gap of 125mm. Other materials may be used to construct the independent leaf, but the principles of structural separation, high mass and airtightness must be maintained. It should also be noted that the method results in the loss of up to 150mm of perimeter floor space which, in smaller buildings, may necessitate the use of a narrower clear gap between the new leaf and the existing wall.

Typical improvements using this method will be from 5 to 10dB across the audible frequency range 100–3150Hz.

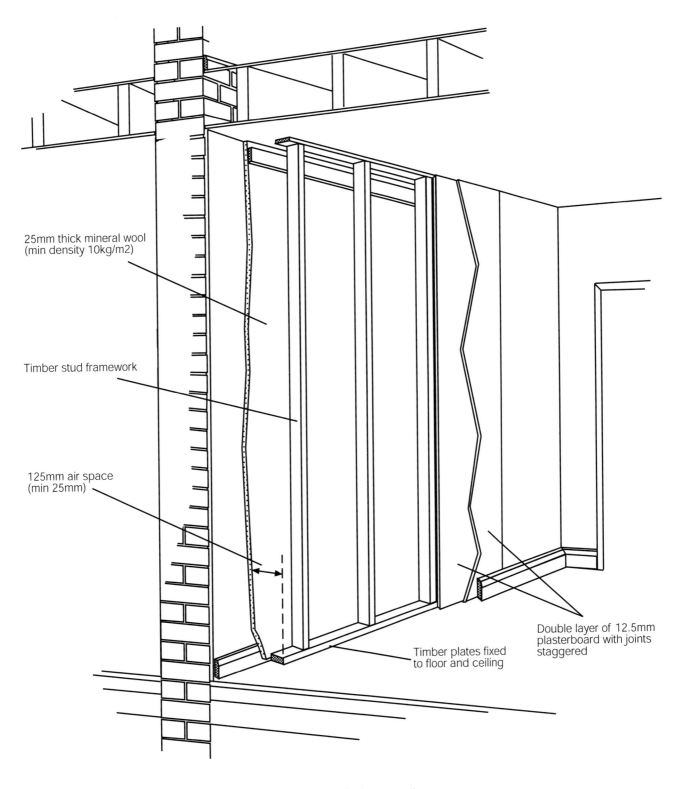

25mm thick mineral wool
(min density 10kg/m2)

Timber stud framework

125mm air space
(min 25mm)

Timber plates fixed
to floor and ceiling

Double layer of 12.5mm
plasterboard with joints
staggered

Fig. 5.1 Acoustic upgrading of separating walls: independent leaf construction

5.3.2 Proprietary metal stud frame independent leaf

Fig. 5.2 shows an alternative proprietary independent leaf construction suitable for the acoustic upgrading of existing separating walls. The Gyproc Independent Wall Lining system consists of a framework of Gyproc 'I' metal studs to which is screwed a single or double thickness of 12.5 or 15mm Gyproc SoundBloc Wallboard. Isowool Batts, 50mm thick, are incorporated into the studding cavity to provide a high standard of sound insulation, and the system is made airtight by the use of acoustic sealant applied between the metal framing and the existing structure.

5.4 Upgrading the acoustic performance of separating floors

Building Regulation E2 requires that any floor separating one dwelling from another dwelling, or from another part of the same building not used exclusively as part of the dwelling, shall resist the transmission of *airborne* sound. Building Regulation E3 requires that a floor above a dwelling separating it from another dwelling, or from another part of the same building not used exclusively as part of the dwelling, shall resist the transmission of *impact* sound. These requirements are explained by Fig. 5.3. Five different methods of upgrading the sound insulation of existing timber separating floors, all of which meet the requirements of the Building Regulations, are described in detail below.

5.4.1 Floating platform floor

One of the most effective ways of upgrading the sound insulation of a separating floor is to float a new, dense, floor surface on a 25mm layer of resilient mineral wool as shown in Fig. 5.4.

- If the existing floorboarding is sound and level, it can be retained; but plain-edged floorboarding, where there are often gaps between the board edges, should be sealed with an overlay of hardboard sheeting. The existing ceiling can also be retained if it is in good condition but should be at least 30mm thick (plasterboard and/or

plaster). If it is less than 30mm thick it should be upgraded to this thickness using plasterboard with staggered joints.

- A layer of mineral wool, 100mm thick, with a density of not more than 36kg/m³, is laid between the joists within the floor void. This entails gaining access to the void by either lifting and relaying the floorboarding, or, where applicable, during replacement of the existing ceiling if this proves necessary.

- 25mm mineral wool, density 60–100kg/m³, is laid over the floorboarding, followed by a layer of 19mm plasterboard laid loose.

- 18mm tongued and grooved chipboard is laid over, and spot-bonded to, the plasterboard with all joints glued.

- A perimeter gap, 10mm wide, must be left around all edges of the new floating floor to prevent sound waves being transmitted from the floor into the walls. For the same reason, a 3mm gap must be left between the skirting and the floating floor surface.

- All airborne sound paths at the ceiling perimeter must be sealed with tape or acoustic sealant. All other airborne sound paths, for example where services penetrate the floor, must also be fully sealed.

- Typical improvements in sound insulation using this method of upgrading will be from 4 to 8dB for airborne sound over the frequency range 100–3150Hz, and slightly better for impact sound.

Two important factors that must be borne in mind when considering the use of a floating platform floor are the increase in loading and the raising of the existing floor level. The additional layers of chipboard, plasterboard and mineral wool will add to the dead loading on the existing floor joists and their ability to carry this extra loading must be verified before installing the new floating floor. Also, the existing floor level will be raised by approximately 65mm, affecting door thresholds, skirtings, services, sanitary fittings, and so on, and the designer must ensure that the associated problems can be resolved before opting for this method of upgrading.

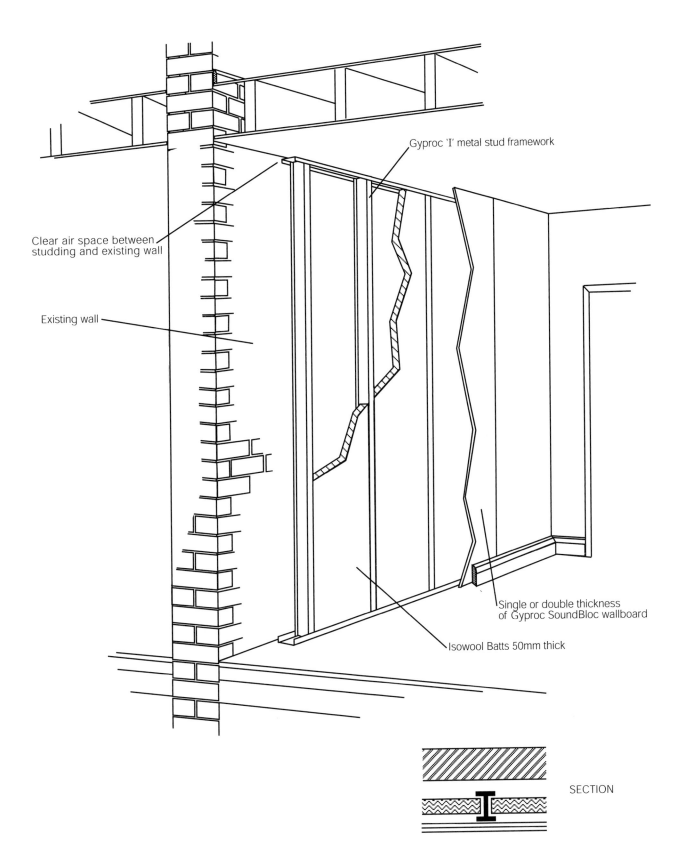

Gyproc 'I' metal stud framework

Clear air space between studding and existing wall

Existing wall

Single or double thickness of Gyproc SoundBloc wallboard

Isowool Batts 50mm thick

SECTION

Fig. 5.2 Acoustic upgrading of separating walls: Gyproc Independent Wall Lining system

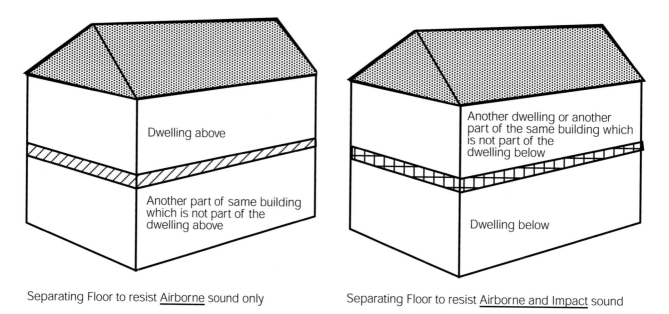

Dwelling above

Another part of same building which is not part of the dwelling above

Another dwelling or another part of the same building which is not part of the dwelling below

Dwelling below

Separating Floor to resist <u>Airborne</u> sound only

Separating Floor to resist <u>Airborne and Impact</u> sound

Fig. 5.3 Acoustic performance of separating floors: Building Regulations Part E requirements

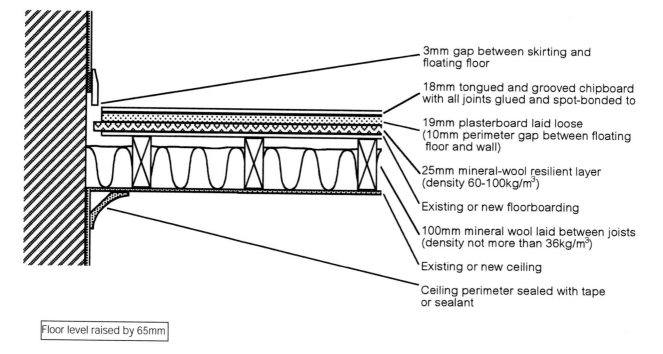

3mm gap between skirting and floating floor

18mm tongued and grooved chipboard with all joints glued and spot-bonded to

19mm plasterboard laid loose (10mm perimeter gap between floating floor and wall)

25mm mineral-wool resilient layer (density 60-100kg/m³)

Existing or new floorboarding

100mm mineral wool laid between joists (density not more than 36kg/m³)

Existing or new ceiling

Ceiling perimeter sealed with tape or sealant

Floor level raised by 65mm

Fig. 5.4 Acoustic upgrading of separating floors: floating platform floor

5.4.2 Floating floor on resilient strips with heavy pugging

This method, shown in Fig. 5.5, entails replacing the existing floorboarding with 18mm tongued and grooved chipboard floated onto 25mm mineral-wool resilient strips laid along the top edges of the existing floor joists.

- The existing ceiling can be retained if it is in good condition but should be at least 30mm thick (plasterboard and/or plaster). If it is less than 30mm it should be upgraded to this thickness using plasterboard with staggered joints.
- The new chipboard surface is made up in sections nailed or screwed to 45mm × 45mm timber

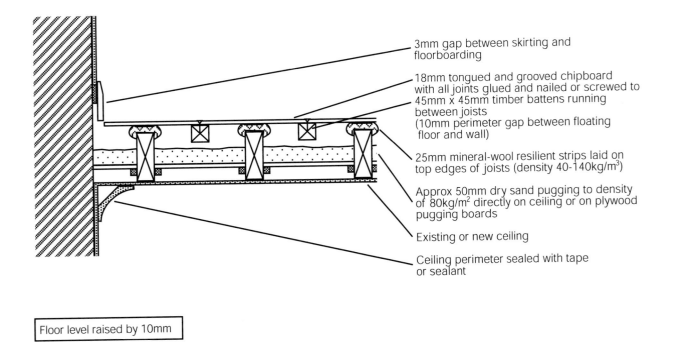

3mm gap between skirting and floorboarding

18mm tongued and grooved chipboard with all joints glued and nailed or screwed to 45mm x 45mm timber battens running between joists (10mm perimeter gap between floating floor and wall)

25mm mineral-wool resilient strips laid on top edges of joists (density 40-140kg/m³)

Approx 50mm dry sand pugging to density of 80kg/m² directly on ceiling or on plywood pugging boards

Existing or new ceiling

Ceiling perimeter sealed with tape or sealant

Floor level raised by 10mm

Fig. 5.5 Acoustic upgrading of separating floors: floating floor on resilient strips with heavy pugging

battens projecting beyond each section to enable adjacent sections to be screwed together when laid. The chipboard flooring is glued along all edges.

- The floor void between the existing joists receives a layer of heavy 'pugging' (or sound-deadening material) to a density of 80kg/m². This may be dry sand (approximately 50mm thick) 2–10mm limestone chips or 2–10mm whin aggregate (both approximately 60mm thick). If there is doubt as to whether the ceiling is capable of supporting the pugging, it should be laid onto plywood pugging boards supported by timber battens fixed to the sides of the joists.

- As with the floating platform floor, a 10mm wide perimeter gap must be left around all edges of the new floating floor, and a 3mm gap left between the skirting and the floor to prevent sound transmission into the walls. The ceiling perimeter must also be sealed, along with all other airborne sound paths.

The principal advantage of this method, in comparison with the floating platform floor, is that the floor level is raised by only 10mm (caused by the 25mm mineral-wool resilient strips crushing down to 10mm).

As with the floating platform floor, this method adds to the dead loading on the existing joists and it is essential, therefore, that their ability to carry the extra loading is checked before any work is carried out.

5.4.3 Proprietary resilient flooring system

Fig. 5.6 shows the Gyproc SI Floor – a proprietary sound-insulating flooring system suitable for upgrading existing timber-joisted floors to sound-resisting floor standard.

- After removing the existing floorboarding, continuous metal channel sections, with integral resilient strips, are fitted over the tops of the existing floor joists and located on plastic clips. Gyproc Plank (plasterboard), 19mm thick, is cut and fitted between the joists, its cut ends resting on the channel flanges.

- Isowool General Purpose Mineral Wool Roll, 100mm thick, is laid between the joists and resting on Gyproc Resilient Bars, fixed to the underside of the joists.

- A double-layer ceiling lining of either Gyproc

Plank and 12.5mm Gyproc Sound Bloc (high-density plasterboard), or two layers of 15mm Gyproc Sound Bloc, is screw-fixed to the resilient bars.

- The floor is completed by screw-fixing 21mm thick floorboarding (softwood or chipboard) through the Gyproc Plank into one flange of the metal channel section.

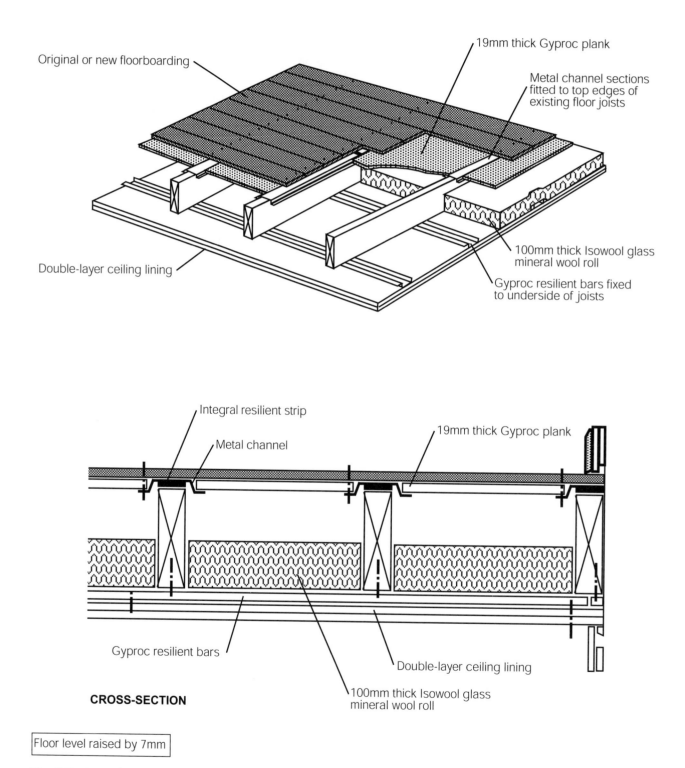

Original or new floorboarding

19mm thick Gyproc plank

Metal channel sections fitted to top edges of existing floor joists

100mm thick Isowool glass mineral wool roll

Double-layer ceiling lining

Gyproc resilient bars fixed to underside of joists

Integral resilient strip

Metal channel

19mm thick Gyproc plank

Gyproc resilient bars

Double-layer ceiling lining

100mm thick Isowool glass mineral wool roll

CROSS-SECTION

Floor level raised by 7mm

Fig. 5.6 Acoustic upgrading of separating floors: Gyproc SI Floor

The Gyproc SI Floor is simple to install and raises the floor level by only 7mm, significantly less than in the previously described methods.

As with the other upgrading methods, the loading capacity of the existing joists should be checked to ensure they are capable of sustaining the additional weight of the system.

5.4.4 Independent ceiling

The methods described above all affect the existing floor surface and floor void, and all raise the floor level by varying amounts. An alternative means of upgrading the acoustic performance of a separating floor, and one which does not affect the existing construction in any way, is to add a new, independent ceiling beneath it. This should be carried on its own set of joists, and spaced as far below the existing ceiling as possible, with an acoustically absorbent material between the new and existing ceilings. The construction method is shown in Fig. 5.7 and involves the following operations:

- If the existing ceiling is less than 30mm thick, it should be upgraded to this thickness using plasterboard with staggered joints.
- Clear air paths between the existing

floorboarding, which is likely if the boards are plain-edged, should be sealed by overlaying with 3mm hardboard sheeting.

- The new ceiling joists, which are of smaller cross-section size than the floor joists, are fixed beneath the existing ceiling. They can be supported by either notching their ends over timber bearers fixed to the walls, or by metal joist hangers.

- The new independent ceiling, comprising two layers of plasterboard having a total thickness of at least 30mm with their joints staggered, is fixed to the underside of the new joists. The clear gap between the new and existing ceilings should be at least 100mm, and there should be a clear gap of at least 25mm between the top of the new independent ceiling joists and the underside of the existing floor.

- Absorbent mineral-wool quilt, at least 100mm thick, with a density of at least 10kg/m^3, is laid on top of the new ceiling, between the new joists.

- The perimeter of the new independent ceiling should be sealed with tape or acoustic sealant.

- Typical improvements in sound insulation using this method will be from 5 to 10dB for airborne sound over the frequency range 100–3150Hz, and slightly better for impact sound.

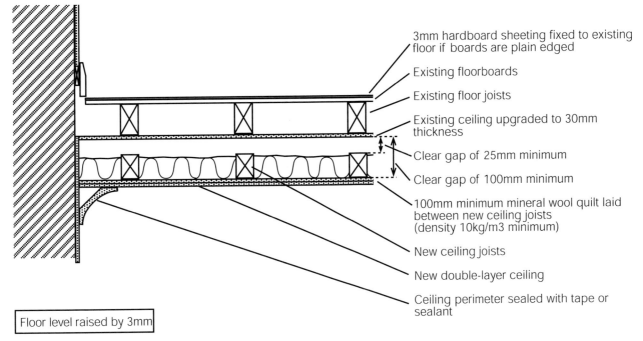

3mm hardboard sheeting fixed to existing floor if boards are plain edged

Existing floorboards

Existing floor joists

Existing ceiling upgraded to 30mm thickness

Clear gap of 25mm minimum

Clear gap of 100mm minimum

100mm minimum mineral wool quilt laid between new ceiling joists (density 10kg/m3 minimum)

New ceiling joists

New double-layer ceiling

Ceiling perimeter sealed with tape or sealant

Floor level raised by 3mm

Fig. 5.7 Acoustic upgrading of separating floors: independent ceiling

It should be borne in mind that the use of an independent ceiling for upgrading sound insulation might no be feasible in all situations. If the existing headroom in the room below is limited, a further reduction of at least 130mm, owing to the introduction of a new independent ceiling, might not be acceptable. The existing ceiling might have an ornate finish, or be an important feature in a listed building, in which case covering it with a new ceiling might not be permissible.

5.4.5 *Proprietary laminated acoustic flooring system*

Fig. 5.8 shows the Akustofloor system, a proprietary laminated sound-insulating flooring system designed for upgrading existing floors to meet Building Regulations requirements – Akustofloor is a registered trademark of Panel Systems Ltd.

- The 2400mm × 600mm laminated Akustofloor panels, comprising 18mm chipboard sheet factory-bonded to a 25mm thick resilient layer of glass fibre, density 112kg/m³, are laid directly onto the existing floorboards with their joints staggered. The chipboard edges of the panels are tongued and grooved, and bonded with adhesive when laid.
- Prior to laying the new flooring panels, the edges of the existing floorboards are sealed with an acoustic mastic, and a self-adhesive, compressible

perimeter strip is fixed to the wall. When laid, the panels should compress this strip by about 2mm to provide a seal against airborne sound.
- When the new Akustofloor panels are fully installed, the skirting boards are refixed to the wall, leaving a gap of 5mm between the bottom of the skirting and the surface of the panels to prevent transmission of impact sound from the floor into the wall.

It should be noted that this method of upgrading raises the original floor level by 43mm, therefore requiring adjustments to doors, skirtings, services, etc.

5.5 Upgrading the acoustic performance of external walls

Upgrading the sound insulation of external walls is rarely necessary, unless the building faces a noisy roadway, factory or other excessive noise source. The importance of upgrading the external walls will also depend to some extent upon the acceptable noise levels within the building, which, in turn, depend on its proposed use after refurbishment. Houses, flats, hotels, hospitals and other buildings where people sleep (or require a minimum of intrusive noise for other reasons) may require the sound-insulation of their external walls upgraded if external noise sources cause, or are likely to cause, problems.

External noise usually enters a building via the windows, since single glazing is a very poor sound

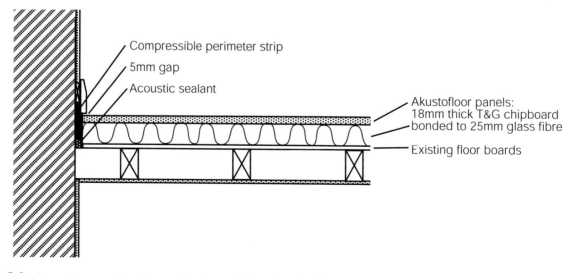

Fig. 5.8 Acoustic upgrading of separating floors: Akustofloor laminated panels

reducer. Relatively insignificant gaps around ill-fitting casements also adversely affect their acoustic performance, and, if a window is opened only slightly, its sound reduction capability will be drastically reduced.

The most effective means of upgrading the acoustic performance of an external wall, therefore, is to deal with the windows. If the existing windows are in good condition, they can be converted into double windows by adding new glazing internally in a separate frame with an intervening airspace of 150–200mm. A narrower airspace will result in a poorer sound-reduction performance. If double windows are installed, it must be ensured that the casements and frames fit tightly. Flexible sealing gaskets should be incorporated between the casements and frames, and gaps between the new secondary frames and the existing window reveals should be sealed with acoustic sealant.

If the installation of double windows is impractical due, for example, to the absence of an adequate reveal in which to fit them, or if the existing windows are in poor condition, the only solution will be to fit replacement windows with double or triple glazing. As with double windows, it is essential that all clear airpaths between casements and frames, and frames and reveals, are properly sealed to prevent leakage of airborne sound. The spaces between the glazing sheets, which should be sealed around their edges, should be as wide as possible to give maximum acoustic upgrading.

Ideally, new double windows or double glazing used to upgrade acoustic peformance should not normally need to be opened since, as previously stated, opening windows drastically reduces their sound-insulation capability. This may, in turn, require the installation of mechanical ventilation which will significantly increase the overall refurbishment costs. In view of this, and the expense of providing and sealing the new windows, acoustic upgrading of external walls in this way should normally only be carried out where intrusive noise from external sources would cause severe problems or loss of amenity for the occupants.

References

Building Research Establishment (1985) *Improving the Sound Insulation of Separating Walls and Floors* (Digest 293), BRE, Watford.

Building Research Establishment (1988) *Sound Insulation of Separating Walls and Floors, Part 1: Walls* (Digest 333), BRE, Watford.

Building Research Establishment (1988) *Sound Insulation of Separating Walls and Floors, Part 2: Floors* (Digest 334), BRE, Watford.

Building Research Establishment (1993) *Double Glazing for Heat and Sound Insulation* (Digest 379), BRE, Watford.

Building Research Establishment (1999) *Improving Sound Insulation* (Good Repair Guide 22: Parts 1 & 2), BRE, Watford.

Department of the Environment and The Welsh Office (1992) *The Building Regulations 1991 Approved Document E: Resistance to the Passage of Sound*, HMSO, London.

Department of the Environment, Transport and the Regions (1999) *Manual to the Building Regulations*, DETR, London.

Powell Smith, V. and Billington, M.J. (1999) *The Building Regulations Explained and Illustrated*, Blackwell Science, Oxford.

Richardson, B.A. (1991) *Defects and Deterioration in Buildings*, E. & F.N. Spon, London.

Stephenson, J. (1995) *Building Regulations Explained*, E. & F.N. Spon, London.

6
Preventing moisture and dampness within buildings

6.1 General

The most common single cause of building deterioration is dampness, and it has been estimated that over 1.5 million dwellings in the UK are seriously affected by dampness problems. The principal sources of dampness are rainwater penetration through roofs and external walls, rising damp through walls and solid floors, and condensation. Because its causes and prevention are different from other sources of dampness, condensation is dealt with separately.

6.2 Preventing moisture penetration through external walls and walls below ground level

The majority of older buildings have solid stone or brick external walls which are inherently vulnerable to rainwater penetration, often resulting in permanent dampness and deterioration of plasterwork and internal finishes. The severity of the problem varies and, at best, might result in only a few damp patches over the internal surface of the wall. In some cases, however, the dampness may be so severe as to cause total deterioration of plasterwork and finishes over large areas of the wall. Walls below ground level enclosing basement accommodation are permanently vulnerable to groundwater penetration and it is quite likely that such walls in older buildings will not have received any waterproofing treatment when originally constructed. In such cases their internal surfaces and finishes will be subject to dampness and deterioration.

A number of different techniques can be used to overcome the problems of moisture penetration through solid walls, as discussed below.

6.2.1 Internal treatments

6.2.1.1 Dry linings

The use of dry linings for upgrading internal wall surfaces is described in detail in Section 3.2.2. In cases where the external walls are suffering only from slight dampness, a traditional timber batten dry lining, used in conjunction with an externally applied water-repellent solution, is an appropriate means of overcoming the problem. The dry lining is fixed as described in Section 3.2.2 to provide a new, dry wall surface, and additional precautions are taken to protect it from the penetrating dampness. The vertical timber battens must be pressure-impregnated with preservative to prevent the risk of fungal attack, and they should be secured to the wall over strips of polythene sheeting or bitumen felt to isolate them from the damp wall. If the dampness is widespread, the whole wall surface should be lined with a polythene sheet, properly lapped and jointed, and secured to the wall by the timber battens.

Similarly, a metal channel dry-lining system, also described in Section 3.2.2, could be used as an alternative to a timber batten system, to prevent slight damp penetration. The metal channels should be fixed to the wall with Dri-Wall adhesive and the existing wall surface should be treated with a waterproof EVA in the line of the adhesive dabs. The provision of ventilation in the cavity between the new lining and the existing wall is also recommended.

If the damp penetration is more severe, a dry lining fixed directly to the wall will itself be vulnerable to deterioration, and other methods of dealing with the problem must be employed.

6.2.1.2 Pre-formed waterproof sheeting systems

A number of proprietary waterproof sheeting systems are available for application to walls, above and below ground level, which are suffering from moisture penetration.

Newlath 2000 is a damp-proof lightweight sheet material made from high-density polypropylene, 0.5mm thick, formed into a pattern of raised studs linked by reinforcing ribs. The 5mm high studs face the wall, creating channels which allow air to circulate freely behind the Newlath 2000. A polypropylene mesh welded onto the other side of the Newlath 2000 provides a rot-proof key for a plaster finish. The material is inert and highly resistant to water, alkalis, saline solutions, and organic acids, and is not affected by minerals. It is also resistant to bacteria, fungi and other small organisms. Newlath is particularly suited to refurbishment and improvement work where rising and penetrating damp is a serious problem in the existing walls. It is supplied in 1.5-metre-wide rolls, 10 metres in length, and works on the principle of providing a ventilated moisture-proof barrier between the existing wall surface and the new applied finish, as shown in Fig. 6.1.

All damp or crumbling plaster, where it exists, should be removed prior to fixing the Newlath 2000 to the wall surface. The material can then be fixed to the background, using 50mm-long polypropylene plugs at not more than 300mm vertical and horizontal centres. Closer centres should be adopted on uneven or curved surfaces. For fixing to wood or other nailable surfaces, galvanised clout nails can be used. All joints between adjacent sheets should be lapped by not less than 100mm. Newlath 2000 is available in brown or clear polypropylene. The clear version provides the added capability of visually identifying adequate fixing positions in the substrate, especially useful when the latter is of variable materials.

The provision of adequate through ventilation between the Newlath 2000 and the damp wall is essential, and this is achieved by using Newlath Profile Strips along the top and bottom of the wall. The Profile Strip prevents the new finish from making contact with the original surface and stimulates the flow of air to carry away any residual dampness into the atmosphere. The small quantity of moisture involved is easily absorbed into the large volume of air in the room. Use of the profile bead also ensures a constant depth of plaster. If it is not possible to use the profile, ventilation gaps should be provided at both bottom and top. The bottom edge of the Newlath 2000 must be raised 20–25mm above the floor, and a 2–3mm gap left at ceiling level. Once the plaster finish has been applied and has dried, the ventilation gaps can be concealed by a wooden skirting and coving as shown in Fig. 6.1.

Newlath 2000 will accept plasters specified by the manufacturer which should be applied to a thickness of 13–15mm to provide the new, damp-proofed wall finish. In addition to providing a damp-proof base for internal wall finishes, Newlath 2000 can be used for arches and vaults, and also as a base for external render finishes.

An alternative product to Newlath 2000, produced by the same manufacturer, is Newton System 500. This is a high-density extruded membrane, 0.6mm thick with a raised stud formation 8mm high, similar in principle to Newlath described above but capable of withstanding more aggressive groundwater conditions. The material is also suitable for damp-proofing of floors and is described in detail in Section 6.4.

6.2.1.3 Waterproof coatings (cement-based)

A number of proprietary materials are available specifically for brush or spray application to walls suffering from damp penetration both above and below ground level.

Thoroseal, supplied by Master Builders Technologies, is suitable for the interior and exterior waterproofing of brickwork, stonework and concrete above and below ground level including basements. It comprises a blend of Portland cements, well-graded sands and chemical modifiers supplied in powder form. The material is site-mixed with Acryl 60, an acrylic polymer in the proportions of 1 part Acryl 60 to 3 parts water. The wall surface being treated should be completely clean, stucturally sound and mechanically keyed.

The wall/floor joint, which, in basements, is usually the point of greatest water ingress, should be cut out, cleaned and filled with Waterplug – a special fast-setting mortar designed to stop water seepage at joints, cracks

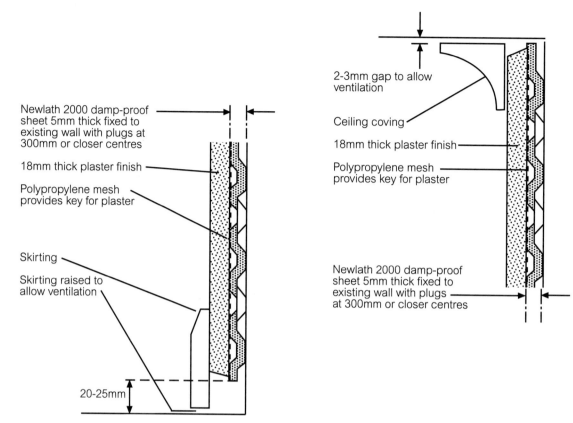

Newlath 2000 damp-proof sheet 5mm thick fixed to existing wall with plugs at 300mm or closer centres

18mm thick plaster finish

Polypropylene mesh provides key for plaster

Skirting

Skirting raised to allow ventilation

20-25mm

2-3mm gap to allow ventilation

Ceiling coving

18mm thick plaster finish

Polypropylene mesh provides key for plaster

Newlath 2000 damp-proof sheet 5mm thick fixed to existing wall with plugs at 300mm or closer centres

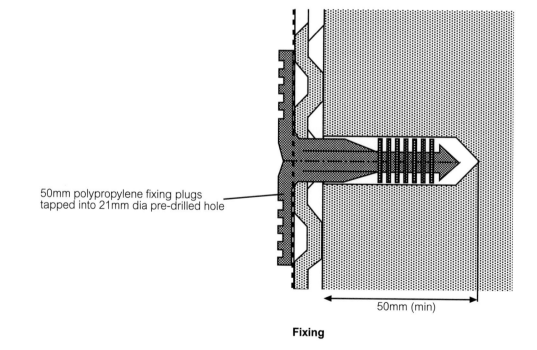

50mm polypropylene fixing plugs tapped into 21mm dia pre-drilled hole

50mm (min)

Fixing

Fig. 6.1   Newlath 2000 damp-proof sheeting

and holes in the substrate. When the Thoroseal has been mixed to a thick batter-like consistency, in the proportions 5.2 litres of Acryl 60/water, to 25 kilogrammes of powder, a first coat is brush-applied to the pre-dampened wall surface. This coat should be well brushed into the surface, a typical application being 1.5mm thick. This first coat should be left at least overnight to cure before applying the second coat to approximately 1mm thickness. Thoroseal is available in grey and white, and, to ensure proper coverage, the second coat should be white over a grey first coat.

The Thoroseal itself may act as the final finish, and can either be textured or given a smooth finish. Alternatively, a cement-based renovating plaster may be applied, in which case the final coat of Thoroseal should be applied with horizontal brush strokes to provide a better key for the finish.

6.2.1.4 Waterproof coatings (bitumen-based)

RIW Liquid Asphaltic Composition is a solution of natural and petroleum bitumens in white spirit applied cold in two coats to form a damp-proof membrane which dries to a uniform gloss black finish. The material can be applied to the internal face of external walls above ground level to prevent moisture penetration, and is also used as a damp-proof membrane to ground floors and for the waterproofing, or tanking, of basements.

All surfaces to be treated must be perfectly clean and dry, to a depth of 1–2mm with any voids or hollows made good to a flush finish with Portland cement mortar. Brickwork or stonework should be sound with joints flush-pointed before the membrane is applied.

The RIW Liquid Asphaltic Composition should be applied by brush, roller or spray in two coats at a minimum application rate of 1.7 litre/m² for the first coat and 2.5 litre/m² for the second. A minimum of 24 hours should elapse before application of the second coat.

Where RIW Liquid Asphaltic Composition is used above ground level to combat penetrating moisture, it can be finished with a direct application of two-coat plaster to the manufacturers' recommendations. Below ground level, where penetrating moisture is subject to hydrostatic pressure, a masonry supporting wall is required. A wall of brick, block or concrete should be constructed immediately after the membrane has cured. If brick or block is used, a cavity should be left between the membrane and the loading skin, and the cavity filled with mortar as the work proceeds. Fig. 6.2 shows the application of RIW Liquid Asphaltic Composition both above and below ground level.

6.2.1.5 Waterproof coatings (urethane-based)

An alternative to RIW Liquid Asphaltic Composition, produced by the same manufacturer, and suitable where the situation demands a higher-performance waterproofer, is RIW Flexiseal. This is a solvent-free thixotropic liquid based on urethane pre-polymers which, on contact with atmospheric moisture, cures to give a tough rubber-like coating. The material is applied in the form of a blue basecoat and a black topcoat by brush, roller or spray. Finishing and protection is the same as for RIW Liquid Asphaltic Composition, described above.

6.2.1.6 Traditional dense polythene membrane wall linings

As an alternative to the use of the dry-lining and proprietary waterproofing systems described above, moisture penetration can be successfully prevented using the more traditional solution of applying impermeable dense polythene sheeting to the inner surface of the wall. The sheeting, which must be lapped and taped at all joints, is held in place against the wall surface whilst a brick, block or concrete loading wall is erected to protect and support it. If brick or block is used, a cavity should be left between the sheeting and the new loading skin, and the cavity filled with mortar as the work proceeds. This technique is generally only used in basements and is shown in Figs. 6.3 and 6.4. Note the loss of floor space inherent in using this technique. The figures also show the use of a thermal board dry lining (see Section 4.3.1) applied to the new loading skin to upgrade the thermal performance of the existing basement walls.

6.2.2 External treatments

6.2.2.1 Water-repellent solutions

A number of proprietary water-repellent solutions are available, and these provide a relatively simple and inexpensive means of preventing rainwater penetration through external walls when the problem is not too severe. Liquid Plastics K501 Masonry Waterproofing

Solution is a water-based silane siloxane compound specifically designed to provide waterproofing to external building surfaces above ground level. After application the solution is virtually invisible, therefore preserving the natural appearance and texture of the substrate being waterproofed.

K501 is a surface-impregnating solution for porous substrates such as brick and stone, and penetrates from 1 to 4mm into the surface pores, rather than coating the surface, giving it good protection from abrasion, weathering and ultra-violet deterioration. This water-repellent lining to the surface pores prevents capillary

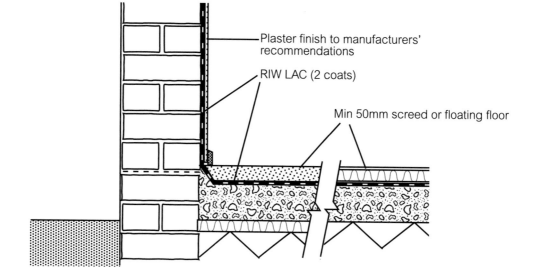

Plaster finish to manufacturers' recommendations

RIW LAC (2 coats)

Min 50mm screed or floating floor

Walls above ground level

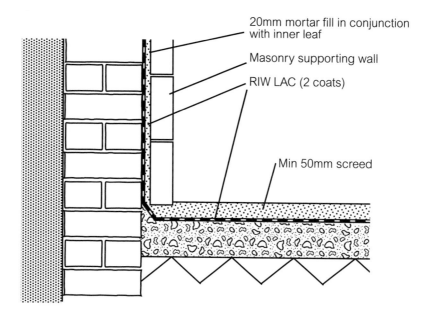

20mm mortar fill in conjunction with inner leaf

Masonry supporting wall

RIW LAC (2 coats)

Min 50mm screed

Walls below ground level

Fig. 6.2 RIW Liquid Asphaltic Composition waterproofing

Fig. 6.3 Traditional dense polythene wall lining with blockwork loading wall and thermal board dry lining. (Note: the untreated section of wall is above ground level)

Fig. 6.4 Traditional dense polythene wall lining with blockwork loading wall and thermal board dry lining. (Note: the untreated section of wall is above ground level)

absorption of water, providing excellent protection against rainwater penetration for at least 10 years.

K501 is applied in two flooding brush or airless spray coats, the second applied as soon as the first coat is dry. The substrate should be dry, clean and free from surface material such as dirt, dust, grease and organic growth prior to application of the solution.

Cementone Water Seal is a water repellent designed to prevent penetration of rainwater through brickwork, masonry and render above ground level. Prior to treatment, the wall surface should be clean and dry and free from efflorescence, moss, grease, oil and loose dust. Defective guttering and pointing should be made good before application.

Cementone Water Seal is applied in one generous flooding coat using a brush or spray, aiming for a 'run-down' of at least 300mm on surfaces of average porosity. The waterproofer does not darken, stain or alter the appearance or texture of the existing wall surface, and penetrates up to 4mm into the surface, lining the pores with a water-repellent coating and preserving the original porosity. Full waterproofing effectiveness is achieved 24 hours after application.

6.2.2.2 External renders

The application of an external render finish to a building's elevations is a more expensive and time-consuming means of overcoming the problem of rainwater penetration. However, a render finish can also be used to fulfil other upgrading requirements, such as improving the building's appearance, or upgrading the thermal performance of the external walls (see Section 4.3.2). Thus, where upgrading of appearance and/or thermal performance are necessary, in addition to a rainwater penetration problem, it may be convenient and economical to apply a render finish. All of the proprietary exterior thermal insulation systems described in Section 4.3.2, in addition to upgrading the thermal properties and appearance of external walls, will also provide total resistance to rainwater penetration.

6.2.2.3 Waterproof masonry paints

The majority of conventional masonry paints are not capable of providing total resistance to rainwater penetration, and are therefore unsuitable as a means of solving this problem. However, recent developments in paint technology have led to the introduction of exterior coatings that are capable of fully waterproofing external wall surfaces.

Monolastex Smooth, produced by Liquid Plastics Ltd., is a water-borne styrene acrylic co-polymer coating system which, when applied in two coats, will provide full waterproofing to existing wall surfaces for at least 15 years. The paint has excellent bonding properties, is permeable to water vapour, allowing underlying moisture to escape without causing flaking or blistering, is resistant to mould, fungal and algae growth and is elastic, allowing it to accommodate movement. Monolastex Smooth is available in a wide range of matt colours and can be applied by brush, roller or airless spray.

The existing surface should be thoroughly cleaned and free from surface material such as dirt, dust, grease and organic growth prior to application. Porous, absorbent backgrounds, such as brickwork or stone, should initially receive an application of Liquid Plastics Bonding Primer.

If a textured waterproof external wall finish is required, Monolastex Textured, produced by the same manufacturer, may be used. This is also a water-borne styrene acrylic co-polymer system and is available in either matt white or magnolia. It is particularly well suited, because of its texture, for hiding surface defects.

Tough-Cote Superflex RW2, produced by Glixtone Ltd., is a water-borne, textured, wholly waterproof decorative wall coating based on an elastomeric resin blended with fine aggregate, titanium dioxide, light-fast earth pigments and special preservative agents. The coating, available in four colours and white, is applied by roller or spray in one or two coats to the substrate which should be thoroughly clean and dry. Porous friable substrates, such as brickwork or stone, should first receive a one-coat application of Glixtone Weatherproof Stabilising Solution SS01. Tough-Cote Superflex RW2 accommodates substantial substrate movement without cracking or loss of bond, is effective at hiding surface defects and, if applied in two coats, provides a decorative protective finish for a minimum of 20 years.

6.3 Preventing rising damp in walls

The penetration of ground moisture, in the form of rising dampness in walls, is a common problem in many old buildings, and it can result from any of the following:

- the lack of a damp-proof course in the original construction
- deterioration and failure of the existing damp-proof course because of age
- bridging of the existing damp-proof course.

Bridging of the existing damp-proof course in an external wall by the building-up of soil, or by the addition of new paving, to a level above that of the damp-proof course, is a common cause of rising dampness. However, this 'short-circuiting' of the existing damp-proof course can easily be alleviated simply by lowering the adjacent soil or paving level back to 150mm below that of the damp-proof course. Provided the damp-proof course is in good condition, the problem will not recur once the residual moisture has dried out from the wall. Other common causes of bridging are where a new external render has been applied and taken over the damp-proof course, or where new mortar pointing has been carried out over the outer edge of the damp-proof course. These also have the effect of 'short-circuiting' the damp-proof course by providing a path for rising moisture to pass around it, but the problems can easily be overcome by cutting back the rendering to above the damp-proof course level, or by raking out the offending mortar-pointing.

The installation of damp-proof courses was made mandatory by the Public Health Act 1875, but in practice their use was not universal immediately. The majority of pre-1900 buildings are, therefore, without damp-proof courses and, as a result, many of them are found to be suffering from severe rising dampness and its associated problems. In such cases, the only means of overcoming the problem is to install a new damp-proof course to cut off further rising ground moisture from entering the building. The installation of a new damp-proof course will also be essential in those older buildings where a damp-proof course was incorporated initially, but where this has deteriorated and failed with age. Damp-proof course failure is quite common in pre-1920 buildings where the felts and slates used for damp-proof courses were often of poor durability, although damp-proof course failure is also not uncommon in more recent buildings.

The installation of a new damp-proof course is both time-consuming and expensive, but it will be imperative in any building suffering from rising dampness caused by the lack of, or failure of, a damp-proof course.

6.3.1 The installation of new damp-proof courses

New damp-proof courses can be installed using a number of different methods:

- The removal of two courses of bricks, a short length at a time, and replacement with two courses of dense engineering bricks. Alternatively the same bricks can be replaced and a new damp-proof course incorporated during the process.
- Physical insertion of a new damp-proof course by cutting a slot in a suitably located horizontal mortar joint and inserting metal sheet, bitumen felt, dense polythene or other suitable material.
- Pressure-injection of a chemical water-repellent fluid into the wall at a suitable position to provide a 'band' of masonry which will resist rising damp.

The first two methods described above are applicable to certain types of wall only: the first method can be used only where the existing walls are of brickwork, and the second method can be used only for walls with continuous horizontal mortar joints and is not, therefore, suited to uncoursed masonry.

Until the early 1980s, the physical insertion of a new damp-proof course into a slot cut into an existing mortar joint was the most widely used means of installing new damp-proof courses. However, the chemical injection method has now overtaken physical insertion techniques and is almost universally used as a means of overcoming rising dampness in walls.

6.3.2 Pressure-injected chemical damp-proof courses

Pressure-injected damp-proof courses involve the use of silicone-resin-based water repellents, or aluminium stearate polymeric water repellents. A large number of proprietary injection systems are available from specialist companies which normally provide a full diagnosis and treatment service. Water repellents work on the principle of lining, rather than blocking, the pores within the material being treated. This allows the passage of some water vapour, but prevents the rise of liquid moisture. The procedures used for the injection of a typical chemical damp-proof course are described below and illustrated in Figs. 6.5 and 6.6.

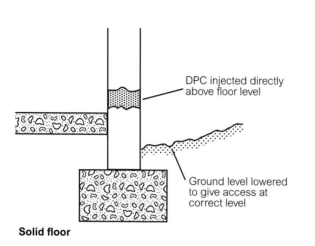

DPC injected directly above floor level

Ground level lowered to give access at correct level

Solid floor

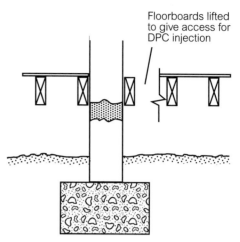

Floorboards lifted to give access for DPC injection

Timber floor/internal wall

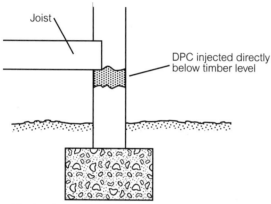

Joist

DPC injected directly below timber level

Timber floor

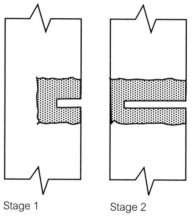

Stage 1   Stage 2

Solid walls 230mm - 460mm thick

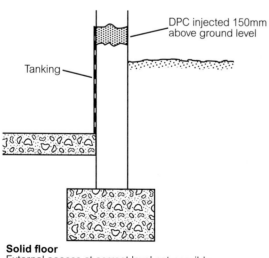

DPC injected 150mm above ground level

Tanking

Solid floor
External access at correct level not possible

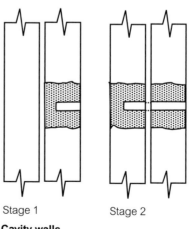

Stage 1   Stage 2

Cavity walls
Two-stage injection procedure

Fig. 6.5 Pressure-injected chemical damp-proof courses

6.3.2.1 Preparation

- Expose the walls externally to at least 150mm below the proposed new damp-proof course level. This may involve digging a trench (see Fig. 6.5).
- Remove all skirtings and floorboards adjacent to the walls suffering from rising dampness and check for timber decay.
- If timber decay is evident, this should be treated and additional underfloor ventilation provided if necessary.
- Cut away the plaster, or other surface rendering, to 450mm above the last visible signs of dampness. If dampness is not evident, expose 230mm of wall along the proposed damp-proof course line.

6.3.2.2 Treatment

- Select the course of masonry to be treated. With a timber floor this should ideally be below the timber level; and, with a solid floor, the course immediately above the floor level (see Fig. 6.5). Avoid engineering bricks or similar dense masonry.
- Drill the holes for injection of the damp-proofing solution. If, owing to ground conditions, access to this course externally is not possible, the injection should take place 150mm above ground level, and the section of wall below tanked internally (see Fig. 6.5).
- Connect the electric pump, feed lines and injector lances to the pre-drilled holes and seal the mouth of each hole (up to six injector lances can be used at once – see Fig. 6.6).

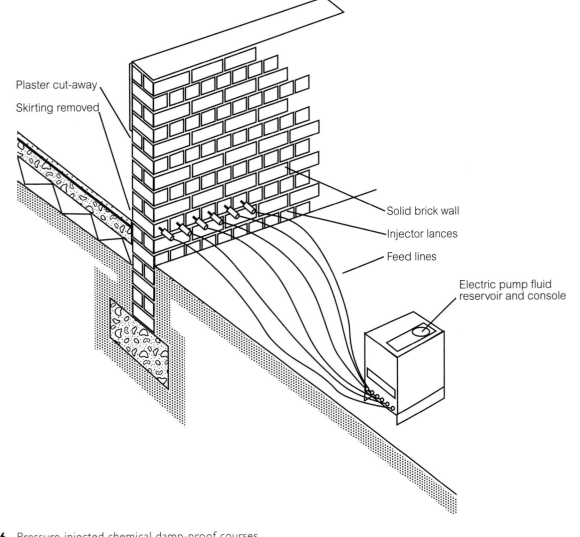

Plaster cut-away

Skirting removed

Solid brick wall

Injector lances

Feed lines

Electric pump fluid reservoir and console

Fig. 6.6 Pressure-injected chemical damp-proof courses

• Open the control valves and commence the pressure injection process. When the section of wall being treated is saturated move to the next set of drillings.

The 9.5mm or 12.7mm diameter injection holes should be drilled horizontally into the wall at the rate of two per stretcher, to a depth of 75mm, and one per header, to a depth of 190mm. For solid brick walls between 230mm and 460mm thick, and for cavity walls, the injection is carried out in two stages, as illustrated in Fig. 6.5. After the outer zone/skin of the wall has been treated, further drilling takes place and the injector lances are passed through the original holes to treat the inner zone/skin. For stone walls the drilling and injection procedures are similar to those for brickwork, with injection holes drilled at 120mm to 150mm centres to a depth of two-thirds of the thickness of the wall. Thicker walls should be treated in two stages as for brickwork.

The walls of many older buildings consist of dry, loose rubble fill between an outer facing and an inner skin, and in order to achieve an effective damp-proof course this infill must be treated separately. After injecting the outer facing and inner skin, separate drillings are made directly through into the rubble, which must be flooded with injection fluid to extend the moisture-resistant band across the full thickness of the wall.

6.4 Preventing rising damp in solid ground floors

In pre-1939 construction, solid ground floors were not normally provided with damp-proof membranes. Floors of concrete, stone flags or quarry tiles in older buildings are therefore often found to be suffering from rising dampness. Originally these floors were not usually covered, and the rising dampness was therefore allowed to evaporate and not cause problems. However, if, in a refurbishment scheme, a new covering is applied to such a floor, evaporation of the rising dampness will be prevented and the covering will rapidly become damp and may ultimately lift and/or deteriorate.

It is therefore essential, first, to check for rising dampness and, if it is present, to provide a new damp-proof membrane before laying the new floor covering. An effective method of checking for rising dampness is to lay a piece of impervious material, such as polythene, on the floor. The underside of the polythene will become wet within a few days if rising dampness is present.

Mastic asphalt or pitch-mastic are suitable materials for damp-proofing solid ground floors. Two 10mm coats should be applied and the coating set into a 25mm × 25mm chase in the wall, bonding with the damp-proof course. Provision of the new damp-proof membrane will usually involve removing existing skirting boards together with the wall coverings and plaster and, possibly, some of the floor edge itself in order to expose the damp-proof course in the wall (where one exists) and bond the new membrane to it to seal the walls and floors completely against rising dampness.

As an alternative to asphalt or pitch-mastic, a proprietary damp-proofing system may be used. The Spry Seal studded membrane system comprises a black, studded sheet of high-density polyethylene 0.6mm thick, supplied in 20-metre-long rolls of 0.5 to 2.4 metres wide. The membrane is laid on the floor with its 8mm high studs against the damp surface, no fixings being required. (Where Spry Seal is applied to walls, sealed nylon fixings are required.) All joints are made watertight with sealing tape prior to laying of the floor surface which may be cement/sand screed, minimum 50mm thick, chipboard sheet, floorboards or other suitable surfacing.

The raised studs provide a ventilated airspace beneath the new floor surface which is vented into the room by leaving gaps at the edges, or to the outside air through airbricks (see Fig. 6.7). If the moisture problem is severe, or running water is present, a completely sealed, unvented, system may be used with drainage gullies or pumps below the membrane.

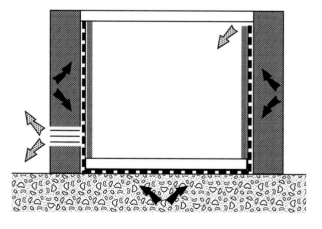

Wall and floor membranes can be joined and sealed to provide protection above and below ground

Fig. 6.7 Spry Seal studded membrane system

The Newton System 500 comprises a high-density extruded membrane 0.6mm thick with 8mm high studs, supplied in rolls. The membrane is laid with its studs against the damp floor surface and fixed using special waterstop plugs inserted into pre-drilled 11mm diameter holes. All joints in the membrane are made watertight with sealing tape before laying of the floor surface which may be a cement/sand screed, minimum 50mm thick, chipboard sheet, floorboards or other suitable surfacing (see Fig. 6.8).

The air gap of 5.5 litres per m² created by the 8mm high studs enables moisture and water vapour to move unhindered in all directions over the whole area of the floor being treated, achieving an equalisation of damp-pressure. This enables the whole area being treated to take the damp loading, rather than only the weakest areas as occurs with conventional damp-proofing systems.

For basement floors, a fully sealed Newton System 500 is recommended with no ventilation to the outside air. Where severe dampness or running water is present

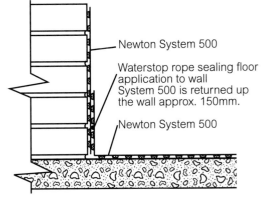

Newton System 500

Waterstop rope sealing floor application to wall System 500 is returned up the wall approx. 150mm.

Newton System 500

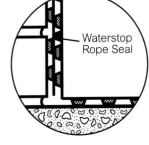

Waterstop Rope Seal

Wall Floor Details on Sealed System

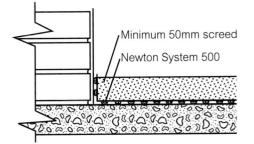

Minimum 50mm screed

Newton System 500

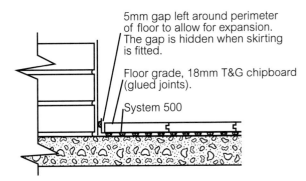

5mm gap left around perimeter of floor to allow for expansion. The gap is hidden when skirting is fitted.

Floor grade, 18mm T&G chipboard (glued joints).

System 500

Fig. 6.8 Newton System 500

or likely, provision for drainage (or sump and pump equipment) will be required. This fully sealed system will also involve applying the membrane to the basement walls. In above ground situations, where the intrusive dampness is not severe, a ventilated Newton System 500 is suitable with venting around the edges at the junction of the floor and walls.

6.5 Preventing rainwater penetration through roofs

Rainwater penetration through the roof of a building, in addition to causing inconvenience to the occupants, often results in deterioration and decay of the roof structure, thermal insulation, ceilings and internal finishes. It is therefore essential in the refurbishment of buildings that existing roofs are thoroughly examined and, in cases where rainwater leakage is evident, that proper remedial action is taken.

6.5.1 *Preventing rainwater penetration through pitched roofs*

A vital barrier against rainwater penetration into pitched roofs is the lining of impervious sarking felt provided immediately beneath the tiles or slates. Any rainwater penetrating the roof covering, because of wind pressure or damaged tiles or slates, is effectively drained away by the sarking felt and prevented from entering the roof space. However, sarking felt has been in use only since around 1938 and, therefore, the roofs of many older buildings, particularly those whose coverings have deteriorated or been damaged, are often found to be suffering from rainwater penetration and its effects.

The only effective solution where there is evidence of rainwater penetration through a roof without sarking felt, is to take off the existing covering, add a new lining of sarking felt, and re-cover the roof. Whether or not the original tiles or slates are re-used will depend on their condition. In many older buildings, the tiles or slates will have deteriorated because of frost, chemical attack or mechanical damage and, generally, if more than 10% of the total are in bad condition, an entirely new roof covering will be advisable.

6.5.2 *Preventing rainwater penetration through flat roofs*

Flat roofs are inherently more susceptible to rainwater penetration because of the much slower rate of run-off. The points most vulnerable to leakage are at flashings, upstands and parapets, at points where openings are formed for soil pipes, flues, and so on, and at joints between separate sheets of the roof covering.

Lead was widely used as a flat roof covering until the late nineteenth century, when it was replaced by zinc, which is lighter and cheaper. The relative lifespans of these materials are 80–100 years and 40 years respectively and, if they are encountered in refurbishment work, it is likely that they will be near the end of their useful life and in poor condition. It is therefore recommended, if an old lead or zinc flat roof is found to be leaking, to strip and entirely replace the covering, since localised repair is likely to give only temporary relief before other faults develop in different parts of the roof.

The flat roofs of more recent buildings are likely to be covered with either asphalt or built-up felt, these materials having lifespans of 20–40 years and 10–15 years respectively. In the event of rainwater leakage, it is possible to carry out localised patch repairs, but these tend to be unsatisfactory and provide only temporary relief. In view of the potentially serious effects of rainwater penetration, it will therefore be advisable, in the majority of cases, to strip the existing roof covering and replace it with a new covering. Alternatively, a new covering can be laid over the existing covering.

Where a roof has suffered from rainwater penetration over a lengthy period, it is likely that associated decay and deterioration of the roof structure and ceilings below will have occurred. It is therefore essential, in addition to repairing or replacing the defective roof covering, that the presence and nature of associated defects is established and that proper remedial work is carried out.

6.6 Preventing condensation within buildings

6.6.1 *The causes and effects of condensation*

Before considering how to prevent condensation, it is necessary to have some understanding of its causes and effects. Water vapour in varying quantities is always present in the air, and the quantity of water vapour that the air can carry depends upon its temperature; the warmer the air, the greater its vapour-carrying capacity. Condensation occurs in a building when warm air, containing water vapour, comes into contact with a cold surface which reduces its temperature and, therefore, its vapour-carrying capacity. Any excess water vapour that the air is incapable of carrying because of its reduced temperature is deposited as condensation on the cold surface.

For any given air condition (temperature/water vapour content) there is a corresponding 'dewpoint temperature'. If air containing water vapour comes into contact with surfaces which are at, or below, this dew-point temperature, it will deposit some of its water vapour as condensation. This usually shows itself as mist, beads of condensation, or damp patches on windows, walls and other surfaces including fabrics, but it will be most obvious on the harder more impervious surfaces.

Condensation can also occur within a permeable building element, where the dewpoint temperature occurs at some point within its thickness, rather than on its surface. This *interstitial* condensation is potentially more harmful than surface condensation, since it is not visible, and the resulting dampness may remain un-detected until substantial decay and damage have been caused.

The adverse effects that are possible as a result of condensation occurring within a building are:

- misting up of windows
- moisture deposited on window frames and sills leading to mould growth and rot
- moisture deposited on wall, floor and ceiling surfaces (most evident on hard, impervious surfaces)
- moisture on and within the surface layers of absorbent surfaces (may not be evident until the surface becomes saturated)
- mould growth on all surfaces affected by condensation
- internal breakdown of materials and elements where interstitial condensation has occurred
- a general deterioration in the internal environment owing to the occurrence of associated dampness, smells caused by mould growth and rot, and deterioration of the appearance of surface finishes.

6.6.2 Preventive measures

Condensation is a widespread problem, and its adverse effects are capable of leaving a building uninhabitable if no preventive measures are in place. It is therefore essential that the following steps are taken when carrying out refurbishment work in order to ensure that condensation does not occur:

- Check for the presence of condensation in the existing building and, where applicable, eliminate it.
- Ensure that the upgrading or replacement of any existing elements does not increase the risk of condensation.
- Where a proposed change of use is likely to introduce new conditions that are conducive to condensation, ensure that appropriate measures are taken to prevent its occurrence.

Condensation is caused by a combination of different factors, but is most likely to occur in those buildings where large quantities of water vapour are produced, such as buildings housing certain industrial processes and, particularly, housing where modern living habits – for example, drying washing indoors and not opening windows – create conditions that are conducive to condensation. The risk of condensation occurring in buildings can be significantly reduced by paying attention to three specific factors, that is, ventilation, heating, and thermal insulation and vapour barriers.

6.6.2.1 Ventilation

Ventilation helps to remove air containing water vapour from the building and is particularly important where large quantities of vapour are released, such as areas housing certain industrial processes, kitchens, bathrooms, showers, etc. Good ventilation is best achieved using powered extractor fans, and their installation is recommended in areas where large quantities of water vapour are produced. In areas where water vapour levels are lower, natural, rather than mechanical, ventilation will usually be satisfactory and this can be achieved by means of openable windows or ventilators.

6.6.2.2 Heating

Adequate heating reduces the risk of condensation in two ways: first, it warms room surfaces, keeping them above dewpoint and preventing surface condensation; and secondly, it increases the moisture-carrying capacity of the ventilated air. Different heating methods vary considerably in their efficiency at reducing condensation. Short periods of high-level heating with no heating in between are conducive to condensation. Whilst the heat is off, the interior surfaces become cold and may fall below dewpoint. The heating periods usually correspond with a significant increase in water vapour production while the building is occupied and this, in conjunction with the cold interior surfaces, aggravates the problem of condensation.

Leaving some rooms unheated while the remainder of the building is heated, increases the possibility of condensation. The cold interior surfaces of the unheated rooms will be susceptible to condensation as warmer air, with a higher vapour content, migrates to them from heated rooms.

Flueless oil and gas heaters release large quantities of water vapour into the atmosphere and their use significantly increases the possibility of condensation.

Continuous background heating of the whole building, used in conjunction with the main heating periods, is the most effective means of preventing condensation, and, where possible, a system which is capable of economically providing this should be installed.

6.6.2.3 Thermal insulation and vapour barriers

Thermal insulation of walls, floors and roofs helps to reduce the risk of surface condensation by ensuring that their internal surfaces are kept above dewpoint temperature. However, the provision of thermal insulation, while preventing surface condensation, can increase the risk of interstitial condensation within the building element. This is because the insulation has the effect of moving the position of the dewpoint temperature from the element's surface to a point within its thickness. Water vapour will then diffuse into the insulation and the element until it reaches the position of the dewpoint temperature, where interstitial condensation will occur. To prevent interstitial condensation, the water vapour must be prevented from diffusing into the insulation and the element, and this is achieved by providing a vapour barrier on the 'warm side' of the insulation.

Several materials are resistant to the passage of water vapour, including certain paints, wallpapers, polythene sheeting, plastic and aluminium foils. In refurbishment work, vapour barriers are often provided pre-bonded to other materials, one of the most common proprietary examples being vapour-check grade Gyproc Thermal Board. This is similar to Gyproc Thermal Board, described in Section 4.3.1, and comprises gypsum wallboard, factory-bonded to a backing of expanded polystyrene insulation, with a vapour-resistant membrane incorporated between the two. These composite boards are widely used to upgrade the thermal performance of existing walls and roofs (see Section 4) and, when fixed, the vapour-resistant membrane is on the warm side of the polystyrene insulation, therefore preventing the passage of water vapour into the insulation and the existing element.

Where existing elements are insulated by other methods (see Section 4), but still require a new internal lining, normal plasterboard with a pre-bonded vapour-resistant membrane can be used. Gyproc Duplex Wallboard comprises gypsum wallboard, capable of direct decoration, with a metallised polyester film on the inner face which provides resistance to the passage of water vapour.

Ideally, the vapour barrier should be continuous over the whole area of the element, but this is difficult to achieve in practice, especially where the above types of material are used. Joints between the boards and holes around pipes, etc. allow some 'leakage' of water vapour, but, in normal circumstances, this should not cause problems. However, in pitched-roof spaces with insulated ceilings, and in 'cold' flat roofs with insulated ceilings (see Section 4.4), the risks of condensation are much greater and additional precautions are essential. In such cases the roof void above the insulated ceiling should be properly ventilated in order to remove any water vapour that succeeds in penetrating joints in the vapour barrier or 'leaking' through holes around pipes, badly fitting loft trapdoors, etc.

Part F of the Building Regulations, which deals with ventilation in buildings and condensation in roofs, requires that 'Adequate provison shall be made to prevent excessive condensation in a roof void above an insulated ceiling', and it is essential that this is complied with if condensation within cold roof voids is to be avoided.

6.6.3 Preventing condensation in pitched-roof spaces

As stated in Sections 4.4 and 6.6.2, the addition of thermal insulation to the ceiling beneath a pitched roof significantly increases the risk of condensation within the roof space. The additional insulation has the effect of lowering the temperature within the roof space and, consequently, increasing the condensation risk as warmer moist air from the building migrates upwards into the roof. The incorporation of a suitable vapour barrier at ceiling level will considerably reduce the amount of water vapour migrating into the roof space, but, in practice, large quantities of vapour will still enter the roof at 'weak points', such as around loft access trapdoors, at ceiling roses and where service pipework penetrates the ceiling. The water vapour entering the roof will condense on any cold surface, such as the sarking felt, or will be absorbed by the timber components of the roof. Over a period of time, this can lead to serious defects, including:

- fungal decay of roof timbers
- deterioration of the roof insulation owing to water dripping off the sarking felt and saturating the insulation material
- short-circuiting of electrical wiring.

The thermal upgrading of existing elements is now a major feature of building refurbishment, with roofs receiving particular attention because of the excessive heat loss that can take place through them. With the majority of existing pitched roofs, the additional insulation is provided at ceiling level, and it is therefore essential that special provision is made to reduce the associated increased risk of condensation and its damaging effects.

The most effective means of reducing the condensation risk within pitched roofs is to provide adequate ventilation, which will remove the water vapour from the roof space before it has the opportunity to condense. It is now mandatory for all new buildings to incorporate roof space ventilators and, in order to alleviate the condensation problem in existing buildings, a number of proprietary ventilators have been developed for installation into existing roofs.

6.6.3.1 Soffit ventilators

Glidevale soffit ventilators have been specifically designed for incorporation into existing roofs during refurbishment work, and two ventilators from the range are described below and illustrated in Figs. 6.9 and 6.10. Note that both types of ventilator should be installed in conjunction with Glidevale Universal Rafter Ventilators to ensure that the ventilation path does not become blocked by the roof insulation material (see Fig. 6.9).

Glidevale twist and lock soffit ventilators (see Fig. 6.9) are manufactured from ultraviolet-resistant injection-moulded polypropylene with an integral insect grille. The 70mm diameter ventilators, available in black, white or brown, are inserted by a simple 'twist and lock' action into 70mm diameter holes formed through the existing soffit board using a special Glidevale hole saw. The soffit ventilators should be inserted at 200mm centres, and, to ensure fully effective and permanent ventilation, they should be used in conjunction with Glidevale Universal Rafter Ventilators, described below.

Glidevale spring wing soffit ventilators (see Fig. 6.10) are manufactured in polypropylene and comprise an integral insect grille and spring clips which enable them to be easily installed into 270mm long × 92mm wide holes sawn through the existing soffit board. The ventilators should be inserted at 1200mm centres, and, to ensure fully effective permanent ventilation, they should be used in conjunction with Glidevale Universal Rafter Ventilators described below.

Glidevale Universal Rafter Ventilators (see Fig. 6.9) are designed for pushing into the eaves to prevent spillage of roof insulation material into the soffit, and consequent blocking of the soffit ventilators (described above). The ventilators, which are effective with both quilt and granular-fill insulation, are available in two sizes to suit 600mm and 400mm rafter spacings. They are manufactured from rigid PVC sheet, formed to provide a series of channels through which air may pass. When pushed into the eaves the ventilators automatically adjust to the correct roof pitch. The quilt or granular-fill insulation is then laid into the ventilators to complete their installation.

6.6.3.2 Tile and slate vents

Eaves-to-eaves ventilation of roof spaces is the most preferable method, and should be employed wherever possible. However, certain types of roof construction do not lend themselves to this solution and it is therefore essential to use some other means of ventilation. A very effective means of providing adequate roof space ventilation, where eaves-to-eaves ventilation is not practicable, is to employ purpose-made tile and slate vents, fixed at strategic positions over the roof area in place of the normal tiles or slates. Glidevale tile and slate vents are manufactured from an ABS/PVCu blend, treated with ultraviolet-resistant polymeric resin,

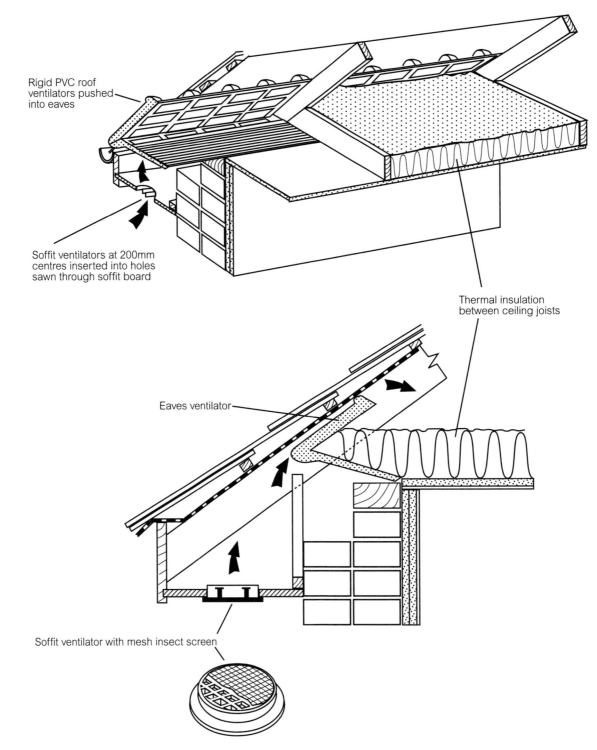

Rigid PVC roof ventilators pushed into eaves

Soffit ventilators at 200mm centres inserted into holes sawn through soffit board

Thermal insulation between ceiling joists

Eaves ventilator

Soffit ventilator with mesh insect screen

Fig. 6.9 Glidevale twist and lock soffit ventilator and roof ventilator

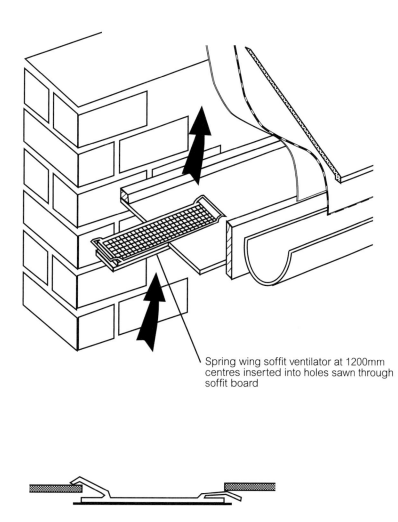

Spring wing soffit ventilator at 1200mm
centres inserted into holes sawn through
soffit board

Installation of spring
wing soffit ventilator

Fig. 6.10 Glidevale spring wing soffit ventilator

and are available in a wide range of sizes, colours, textures and profiles, allowing them to be installed in conjunction with the main tile and slate manufacturers' products. Typical tile and slate vents are shown in Fig. 6.11.

The majority of proprietary tile and slate vents are designed for installation where an entirely new roof covering is being provided, which is not uncommon in refurbishment work. However, if the building in question does not require re-roofing, it will be necessary to insert tile or slate vents individually into the existing roof.

To install a ventilating tile, one existing tile is removed, the sarking felt is cut and folded in a prescribed way, and the new ventilating tile positioned and secured. To install a ventilating slate, it is necessary to remove a number of slates from the area where the vent is to be positioned.

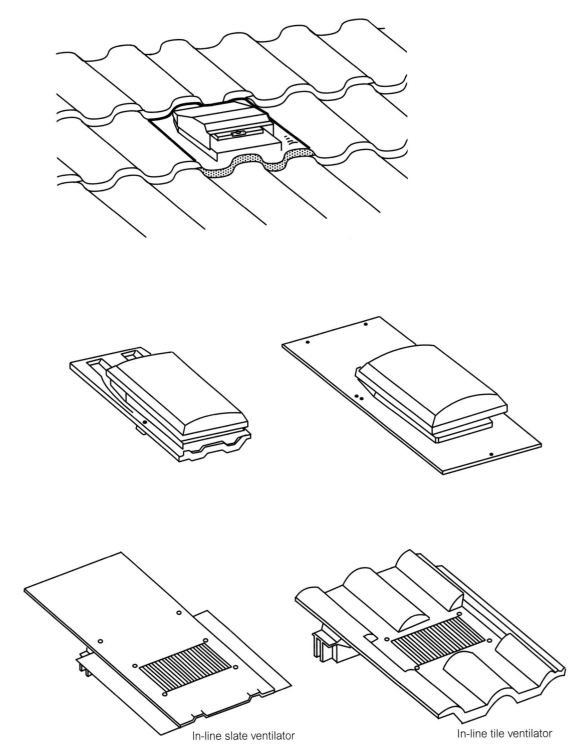

In-line slate ventilator

In-line tile ventilator

Fig. 6.11   Glidevale tile and slate vents

6.6.3.3 Air bricks

A relatively simple, inexpensive means of improving roof space ventilation in buildings where the roof has gable ends, and where eaves-to-eaves ventilation or the installation of tile or slate vents is not practicable, is to insert new air bricks into the gable walls. Air bricks of any standard size can be inserted into the roof's gable ends after carefully cutting out sections of the existing brickwork or masonry, and these will provide a fairly effective means of ventilation. However, this will not be as effective as eaves-to-eaves ventilation.

References

Building Research Establishment (1993) *Damp Proofing Existing Basements* (Good Building Guide 3), BRE, Watford.

Building Research Establishment (1997) *Diagnosing the Causes of Dampness* (Good Repair Guide 5), BRE, Watford.

Building Research Establishment (1997) *Treating Rising Damp in Houses* (Good Repair Guide 6), BRE, Watford.

Building Research Establishment (1997) *Treating Condensation in Houses* (Good Repair Guide 7), BRE, Watford.

Building Research Establishment (1997) *Rain Penetration* (Good Repair Guide 8), BRE, Watford.

Building Research Establishment (1999) *Treating Dampness in Basements* (Good Repair Guide 18), BRE, Watford.

Garratt, J. and Nowak, F. (1991) *Tackling Condensation*, Building Research Establishment, Watford.

Hutton, T. (1998) 'Rising Damp', *The Building Conservation Directory 1998*, ed. J. Taylor, Cathedral Communications Ltd., Tisbury, 38–40.

Newman, A.J. (1988) *Rain Penetration through Masonry Walls: Diagnosis and Remedial Treatment*, Building Research Establishment, Watford.

Richardson, B.A. (1991) *Defects and Deterioration in Buildings*, E. & F.N. Spon, London.

7
Timber decay and remedial treatments

7.1 General

The majority of older buildings contain many more timber components than modern buildings, and it is not unusual to encounter timber decay in refurbishment work, particularly where the building has suffered from neglect and lack of maintenance. The latter often results in the ingress into the building of moisture and dampness which represents one of the principal causes of decay in timber components.

Timber decay can result from fungal attack or insect attack, both of which cause a gradual weakening of the timber, and, if remedial action is not taken, its eventual disintegration.

Where timber decay is evident in a building which is about to be refurbished, it is advisable to call in one of the many companies which specialise in its diagnosis and treatment, such as Rentokil or Terminix Peter Cox. A specialist company will carry out a detailed survey and diagnosis of the timber decay, and provide a treatment and eradication package backed by an extensive guarantee, usually for a minimum of 30 years after treatment.

The nature and treatment of the main forms of timber decay are outlined below.

7.2 Fungal attack

Fungal attack occurs only where sufficient moisture is present in the timber, and it is usually caused by one of two wood-destroying fungi, *Serpula lachrymans* or *Coniophora puteana*.

7.2.1 Dry rot

The best-known wood-destroying fungus is *Serpula lachrymans* or 'dry rot', and this typically grows on timber remaining moist, rather than very wet, over long periods, resulting from moisture penetration into the building, leaking plumbing, or condensation, often combined with bad ventilation (see Section 6). Dry rot has the unique property of being itself able to produce the moisture it needs for further growth, even when the moisture content of the timber has been reduced to below the level needed to sustain fungal growth (around 20%).

The most vulnerable parts of the building include timber ground floors, joists built into solid external walls, and roof timbers. However, all timber within the building will be vulnerable, particularly in the event of a severe attack. Once established in moist timber the fungus will readily extend into adjoining dry timbers and will penetrate masonry and plasterwork in order to reach other sound timber which then, in turn, becomes infected. The fungus grows from very fine airborne spores, rusty red in colour, which have alighted on damp timber, and it gradually spreads, either as a silky white sheet or a greyish felted skin. The fungus feeds on the timber, causing it to lose strength, and reduces it to a dry, brittle state. The rotted timber has a pale brown colour and the surface splits into cuboidal or brick-shaped sections formed by a combination of deep, longitudinal and transverse cracks (see Fig. 7.1). The early symptoms may be a characteristic musty, mouldy smell with, later on, the presence of a rusty red powder (the spore dust) and the appearance of flat mushroom-like growths through joints in the timber.

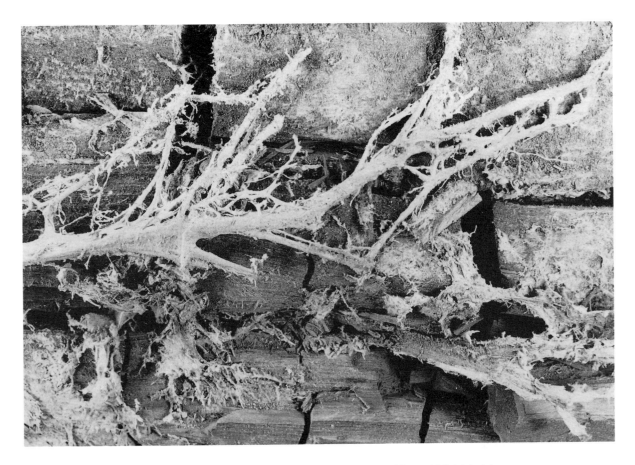

Fig. 7.1   Deep cuboidal cracking resulting from dry rot attack. (Courtesy of Rentokil Initial plc)

7.2.1.1 Treatment of dry rot fungus

Because dry rot is so prolific and capable of spreading through other materials and attacking dry timber, its eradication treatment involves not only the replacement of all affected wood with pre-treated timber, but also the treatment of adjoining timbers, brickwork, plasterwork and adjacent areas well away from the point of decay. All of the following operations must be carried out in order to ensure that the fungus is completely eradicated:

- Locate and eliminate the dampness responsible for the original dry rot attack. This may involve providing a new damp-proof course, preventing moisture penetration through walls, repairing leaking roofs and plumbing, eliminating condensation, clearing the bridging of damp-proof courses and improving ventilation, including the provision of additional airbricks, etc.
- Cut out, remove from the site and burn all defective timbers showing cuboidal cracking, pale-brown coloration, white fungal mycelium or soft areas when probed. All apparently sound timber within 1 metre of defective timber should also be cut out, removed and burned, together with all debris and loose material within roof voids, sub-floor voids and other areas in the vicinity of the attack.
- Carry out a thorough check of all other timbers within the building to which the fungus might have spread. This may involve removing skirtings, architraves, wall panels or ceilings, lifting floorboards, etc.
- Strip off all wall plaster which may contain fungal strands to 1 metre beyond the observed limit of growth, and clean down all exposed masonry by wire brushing. Remove all stripped plaster, debris and dust from the site.
- Sterilise all masonry within 1 metre beyond the observed limit of fungal growth by first applying a blowlamp until the surface is too hot to touch and, secondly, by treating the masonry with a proprietary fungicidal solution.

- Replace all timber that has been cut out with new, well-seasoned timber which has been pre-treated with fungicidal preservative by brush, spray or, preferably, full immersion or vacuum treatment.
- Treat all sound timber within 2 metres beyond the observed limit of fungal growth with fungicidal preservative, applied liberally by brush or spray.
- Make good all work that has been disturbed during investigation, treatment and eradication of the dry rot attack, including renewing stripped plasterwork, decorative finishes, etc.

7.2.2 Wet rot

Coniophora puteana or 'wet rot' is the other common wood-destroying fungus, and this requires much wetter timber than dry rot in order to develop. It is therefore more common in exterior joinery exposed to rain, such as windows, fascia boards, timber cladding, etc., although interior timbers that have become wet because of excessive moisture penetration or leaks in plumbing are also vulnerable.

Unlike dry rot, the wet rot fungus is incapable of spreading to, and infecting, dry timber, and outbreaks are therefore confined to the affected wet timber and its immediate vicinity. In an advanced stage, the wet rot fungus produces slender, thread-like, dark brown or black strands, and there are seldom any signs of a fruiting body or of the olive-brown spores. The decayed timber is dark in colour, and any cracking is less deep than in timber affected by dry rot (see Fig. 7.2).

7.2.2.1 Treatment of wet rot fungus

Because wet rot is not as prolific as dry rot, its outbreaks usually being much more localised, treatment and eradication are simpler, and usually only involve replacement of the affected timber with new pre-treated timber, together with the elimination of the original cause of the wet rot attack.

Fig. 7.2 Shallow cracking resulting from wet rot attack. (Courtesy of Rentokil Initial plc)

A wet rot attack can be remedied by cutting out the affected wood well back from the point of decay, and splicing-in new, preservative-treated timber. However, where the attack is widespread, as is often the case with neglected window frames, localised repair is often not justified, and complete replacement with new units will be preferable. Where the existing windows are badly rotted, their replacement with 'maintenance-free' metal or PVCu units is advisable, since these will neither rot, nor require the expense of regular painting throughout the life of the refurbished building.

Where exterior woodwork has suffered an attack of wet rot, the usual cause is breakdown of the protective paint finish, allowing rainwater to penetrate the timber and create suitable conditions for attack. In the case of internal elements, the cause is usually water penetration through the building envelope, or leaking plumbing, and, in addition to replacing the rotted timber, it is essential that the source of the water or moisture is ascertained and eliminated in order to rule out the risk of further outbreaks.

7.3   Insect attack

The symptoms of insect attack are disfigurement of the timber's surface by small circular- or oval-shaped holes, accompanied by deposits of bore dust, and a gradual reduction in strength. Although insects will attack dry timber, it will be more vulnerable if it is damp, or weakened by fungal decay.

Wood-boring insects lay their eggs on the surface or in crevices in timber and, after the larvae hatch out, they bore into the timber, feeding on it and growing in the process. After a period of between one and several years, the larvae pupate near the surface of the timber, and the beetles emerge, leaving a hole which is characteristic for the particular species of insect. The exit holes are usually clear, sharp edged, and accompanied by bore dust and are thus not easily confused with man-made nail or pin holes.

The most prevalent wood-boring insect is the Common Furniture Beetle (see Figs. 7.3 and 7.4), which is responsible for around three-quarters of all cases of insect attack in buildings. The insect's name is misleading, since it attacks all structural timbers, both hardwood and softwood. Its exit holes are circular, and about 1.5mm in diameter.

Wood-Boring Weevils, responsible for around 5–6% of all cases of insect attack, usually attack very damp or decayed hardwoods and softwoods, often where fungal decay is also present. The exit holes are oval- or slit-shaped with ragged edges and are only ½–1mm wide.

The Death Watch Beetle (see Figs. 7.5 and 7.6), which accounts for about 5% of all cases of insect attack, leaves larger exit holes, approximately 3mm in diameter, but attacks only hardwoods, and particularly oak. It is therefore usually found only in much older buildings where the use of oak was common.

The *Lyctus* Powder Post Beetle also attacks only hardwoods, including oak, ash and particularly elm. Its exit holes are circular, and 1–2mm in diameter, and its bore dust is a fine talcum-like powder, distinguishing it from that of the Death Watch Beetle, which produces a much coarser dust.

The House Longhorn Beetle attacks only softwoods and its area of activity is restricted to the South of England. The insect causes rapid deterioration of the timber it attacks, leaving very large oval exit holes of approximately 9mm x 5mm in size. This insect and the *Lyctus* Powder Post Beetle are together responsible for only about 1% of all cases of insect attack.

7.3.1   Treatment of insect attack

Where the extent of the insect attack is not advanced, usually indicated by few and scattered exit holes, causing negligible reduction in the strength of the timber, it is recommended that the timber be treated with either brush- or spray-applied insecticide. This will kill any insects that are still active and leave the wood toxic to wood-boring insects, therefore preventing further attack. All apparently unaffected timbers within the building should also be treated with insecticide, on the assumption that insects have emerged and laid eggs elsewhere, the adverse results of which might take several more years to appear. Modern proprietary insecticides are capable of penetrating timbers deeply, and being retained by the wood for very long periods, irrespective of other causes of deterioration, and, if properly applied, will ensure the timber remains toxic to wood-boring insects for 30 years or more.

Timbers that have been structurally weakened by insect attack must either be treated with insecticide and

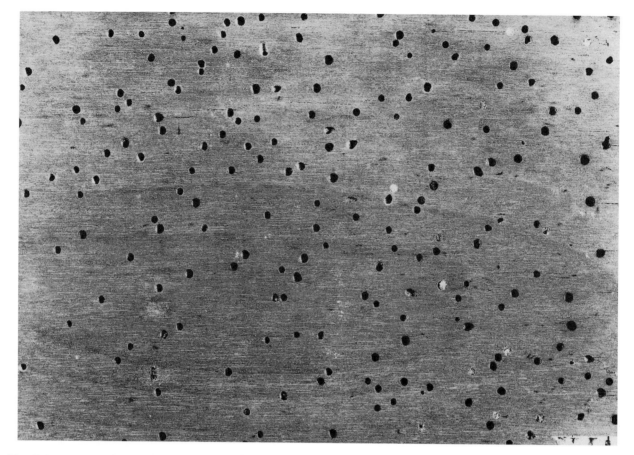

Fig. 7.3 Furniture Beetle exit holes. (Courtesy of Rentokil Initial plc)

Fig. 7.4 Furniture Beetle damage. (Courtesy of Rentokil Initial plc)

Fig. 7.5   Death Watch Beetle larva. (Courtesy of Rentokil Initial plc)

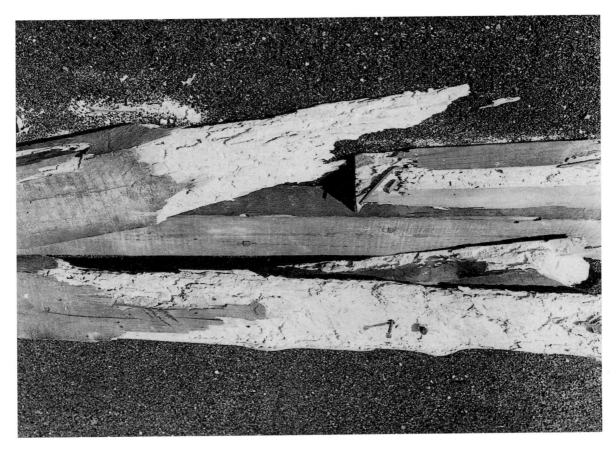

Fig. 7.6   Death Watch Beetle damage. (Courtesy of Rentokil Initial plc)

strengthened, or cut out, burned and completely replaced with new, pre-treated timber. Particular attention should be paid to structural timbers in roofs and floors. In addition, all apparently unaffected timbers within the building should receive full insecticide treatment.

Because many older buildings are likely to have suffered from both insect and fungal attack, it is advisable, when carrying out a programme of treatment and eradication, to use one of the more recently developed 'combination fluids', which contain both insecticide and fungicide. If the treatment is thorough, this should ensure that further decay of any description will not occur in the building for at least 30 years, after which retreatment will be advisable.

7.4 In-situ injection techniques for the preservation of timber components

The in-situ injection of preservatives into timbers that have been affected by, or are susceptible to, fungal and insect attack is a relatively recent development. Where fungal or insect attack in timber components is not sufficiently advanced to have caused a significant loss in strength, specially designed plastic nozzles, inserted into the timber, can be used to pressure-inject preservatives much more deeply than can be achieved by surface application. The technique can also be used on components that have not suffered attack, but which are considered vulnerable.

The minimum size of timber that can be treated by in-situ injection is 50mm x 25mm, and typical applications include external softwood joinery, such as window and door frames, floor joists, roof timbers, beams and lintels.

In the Wykamol timber injection system (see Fig. 7.7), hollow polypropylene injectors (36mm long x 9.5mm diameter, or 24mm long x 6.5mm diameter) are inserted into pre-drilled holes in the timber. The injector holes must penetrate to within 12mm of the component's far face and be at least 40mm deep for the larger injector, and 30mm for the smaller. The outer end of each injector has an injector nipple containing a non-return valve which is left protruding from the face of the timber, and to which the injection line and pump is attached. The organic preservative fluid is then injected under pressure for at least two minutes, or until the timber is seen to be saturated.

The positions and number of polypropylene injectors required will vary according to the type and size of component being treated. For example, a 200mm x 75mm beam on edge would require injectors inserted at 300mm staggered centres in two rows 35mm from the top and bottom edges of the wide face; or, where the upper narrow face is accessible, in one row at 300mm centres (see Fig. 7.7). Small-section external softwood joinery, such as window and door frames, can be treated using the smaller, 24mm long injectors, which should be inserted from the exterior in areas susceptible to decay, such as the lower and intermediate joints of frames, including sills. They should be inserted into each member at a distance of approximately 64mm from each side of the joints and, if required, at regular centres between joints.

After the injection procedure has been completed, the injector nipple can be cut off flush with the surface, and the holes sealed with putty and matching paint. Alternatively, the injectors and nipples can be driven fully into the timber and plastic sealing caps inserted. In particularly high risk areas, where appearance is not important, the injector nipples can be left intact, allowing further injections of preservative fluid in the future where this is considered necessary. However, under normal circumstances, this technique of timber preservation should ensure that sections are free from fungal and insect attack for at least 10 years after treatment. Ideally, the injection treatment should be combined with normal painting maintenance and repairs to stop further decay in affected areas and protect sound joints from attack. Injection of the organic preservative does not impart strength to rotted wood or render unnecessary the application of normal standards in deciding the extent of repairs and/or replacements, which would always precede the protective injection where necessary.

An alternative timber injection treatment to the above employs preservative in the form of a gel. Wykamol Boron Gel 40 is a glycol-based wood preservative containing disodium octoborate, designed for injection into larger-section timbers, such as beams or joists, to protect against fungal and insect attack. The gel can be used to treat sound (new or existing) timbers or timbers where decay is already present, provided sources of moisture are removed and ventilation improved. It is not suitable for timbers exposed as a decorative feature as the gel causes staining to the timber and to adjoining porous materials.

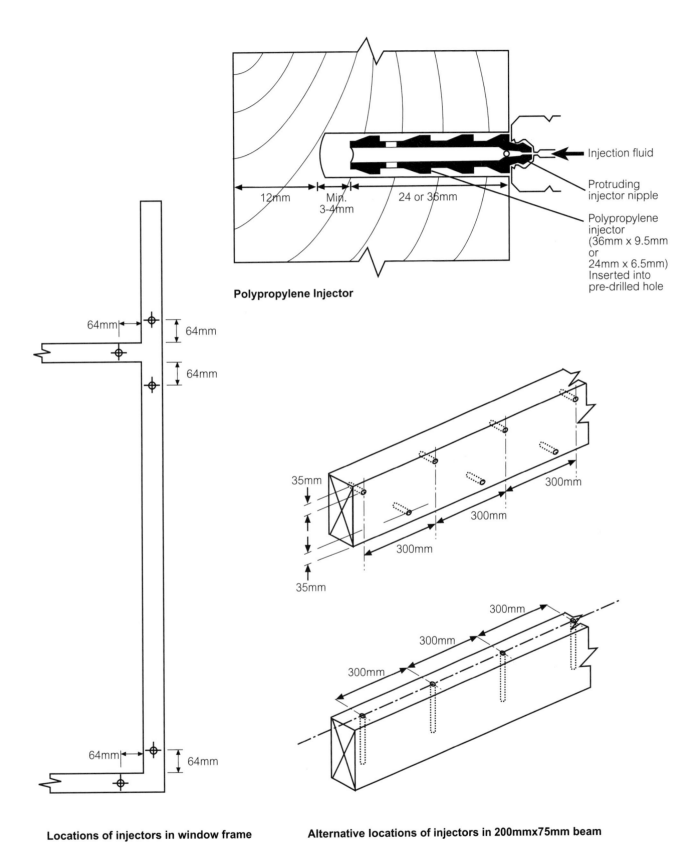

Polypropylene Injector

Injection fluid

Protruding injector nipple

Polypropylene injector (36mm x 9.5mm or 24mm x 6.5mm) Inserted into pre-drilled hole

12mm

Min. 3-4mm

24 or 36mm

64mm

64mm

64mm

64mm

64mm

35mm

35mm

300mm

300mm

300mm

300mm

300mm

300mm

300mm

Locations of injectors in window frame   **Alternative locations of injectors in 200mmx75mm beam**

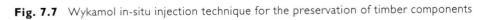

Fig. 7.7 Wykamol in-situ injection technique for the preservation of timber components

The 10mm diameter injection holes are drilled to within 15mm of the full depth of the timber at intervals and spacings according to the size of section. After injection of the gel the holes are sealed with plastic plugs or timber dowelling.

An alternative to the above fluid- and gel-injection systems involves the use of boron rods which are implanted into the timber sections where there are signs of decay, or earlier as a preventative measure. PJG Boron Rods are cylindrical rods composed of anhydrous boric oxide. They contain the maximum level of borate preservative available in rod form. The preservative, which controls both insect and fungal attack, is mobilised when exposed to a moisture content in excess of 25% within the timber. Typical applications are for timbers which may be exposed to wetting in service, such as windows and external doors. The rods are inserted into pre-drilled holes approximately 1–2mm greater in diameter, and at least 10mm longer than the rods used. The holes should extend to not more than 10mm from the rear face of each timber section being treated. Once inserted, the rods are sealed in position with a suitable filler, plastic cap or timber dowelling. Standard rods are 8mm x 65mm long; other sizes being available to order. The number and configuration of the rods, and their installation, must be in accordance with the manufacturer's instructions.

7.5 Localised repair techniques for decayed timber window frames and other joinery

Timber window frames are highly susceptible to wet rot attack and subsequent localised decay, and it is not unusual to find extensive damage to window frames in older buildings, particularly where maintenance has been neglected.

Provided the areas of decay are not too extensive, and the larger proportion of timber remains unaffected, it is possible to carry out localised repair to good effect. The Cuprinol Ultra Tough Wood Filler system for localised repair of decayed timber windows and other joinery is a polyester resin-based filler which hardens when mixed with catalyst paste. It hardens by chemical action and is fast-setting, non-shrink and weather-resistant with excellent adhesion to wood. It can be sanded, filed, drilled, screwed and nailed and is sufficiently flexible to accommodate small movements in the surrounding wood without loss of bond at the filler/timber interface. Ultra Tough Wood Filler is available in natural and white, and its application involves the following operations:

- Identify the full extent of any decay by probing the wood with a sharp instrument. Cut out all badly decayed and very soft wood.
- Remove paint, varnish, dirt or loose material from the area for repair and immediately around it. If the wood is wet, allow to dry thoroughly.
- Apply Cuprinol Rapid Drying Wood Hardener, an organic solvent-based liquid containing wood-hardening components, to the repair area. The hardener should be applied liberally by brush in two or three coats, allowing each to be absorbed before the next is applied. To maximise long-term preservation of the timber, the repair area should be pre-treated with Cuprinol Wood Preserver Clear, an all-purpose preserver for the protection of sound wood against rot and woodworm.
- To obtain improved anchorage of the filler in deep holes greater than 25mm, screws should be inserted into the base of the holes leaving the heads and stems exposed inside the holes.
- Mix Wood Filler with catalyst in the proportions indicated on the pack. The mixed filler remains usable for approximately 10 minutes, the setting time reducing in warm weather and increasing in cold weather. Apply a thin coat of mixed filler to the repair, pressing well in to obtain good adhesion. Immediately fill in the remainder of the hole, leaving slightly proud for sanding down.
- The filler will set hard in approximately 30 minutes under normal conditions, after which it can be smoothed to the required profile using sandpaper or a file. The repair can then be finished with either paint or woodstain.

Where maintenance has been neglected over an extensive period, window frames will not be the only timber elements that are vulnerable to decay, and this technique is equally applicable to the localised repair of other components such as doors and frames, claddings, fascia boards, etc.

7.6 Decay of structural timbers

As discussed in Section 7.1, intrusive moisture is one of the principal factors that can lead to timber decay, the most vulnerable structural elements being roofs and floors.

Sarking, the universally accepted second line of defence against rainwater penetration through roofs, has only been in general use since around 1938 and thus the roof structures of many older buildings are highly vulnerable. Any damage to, or lifting of, tiles or slate coverings permits direct rainwater penetration into the roof timbers, often resulting in the onset of fungal attack. Particularly vulnerable are the ends of roof trusses and rafters which will need repairing or strengthening if ultimate collapse of the roof is to be avoided. Roof truss and rafter ends are also vulnerable if rainwater gutters become blocked, since the overflow is invariably absorbed into the top of the wall in the vicinity of where these timbers are built in.

Ground floors in older, solid-walled buildings are vulnerable to rising dampness into the brickwork or masonry surrounding the ends of built-in floor joists. Although the use of DPCs was made mandatory by the Public Health Act of 1875, their use did not become universal until around 1900 and, even where they were installed, they may well have deteriorated. It is also not unusual to encounter failed DPCs in more recent buildings. Built-in floor joists or beams in buildings where DPCs are non-existent or have failed are, therefore, often in need of replacement or repair owing to moisture-related decay. The ends of upper-floor joists and beams are also vulnerable to rainwater penetration directly through solid walls, and to other causes of intrusive dampness because of, for example, broken downpipes or leaking gutters which can result in walls becoming drenched with large volumes of water.

7.7 Mechanical repair of decayed structural timbers

Where structural timber members, such as floor beams, joists and roof trusses, have suffered decay to the extent that they are structurally weakened, it will be essential either to replace or repair them. Unless the building has been seriously neglected and exposed to the elements for a prolonged period, any timber decay will tend to be only localised. For example, beams, joists and roofing members will generally be decayed only at their ends where they are built into supporting walls, since it is here that they are most vulnerable. The bulk of the member is likely to be perfectly sound and unaffected by decay and therefore it will make economic sense to repair only the decayed parts, rather than undertaking a complete replacement.

The traditional, and still most widely used, techniques for repairing decayed structural timbers involve introducing steel angles, channels or plates, often combined with the splicing-in of new timber in order to replace or strengthen those parts which can no longer fulfil their structural function.

7.7.1 Repair of decayed joist and beam ends

Where the decay is restricted to the extreme end of the joist or beam, that is, only that part which is built into the supporting wall, and no decay has spread into its exposed section, the member can be cut off flush with the wall surface and steel supports used to reconnect it to the wall. In such cases, it is highly likely that the timber wall plate will also have suffered decay and this will therefore need to be removed and replaced. The steel supports are mechanically connected to the end of the joist or beam using bolts and normally cast into a new concrete padstone built into the wall.

Fig. 7.8 shows the use of a steel joist hanger and steel straps connected to the end of the joist or beam and cast into a new concrete padstone.

Fig. 7.9 shows the use of through-bolted steel channels on each side of the joist or beam cast into a new concrete padstone.

In both cases the remaining unaffected parts of the joists or beams should receive brush or spray preservative treatment for a minimum of 2 metres from the decayed areas.

7.7.2 Repair of decayed roof truss ends

Where decay has occurred in the ends of timber roof trusses, and if it has resulted in serious loss of strength, there will be no choice but to replace the decayed parts with new, preservative-treated timber. This involves

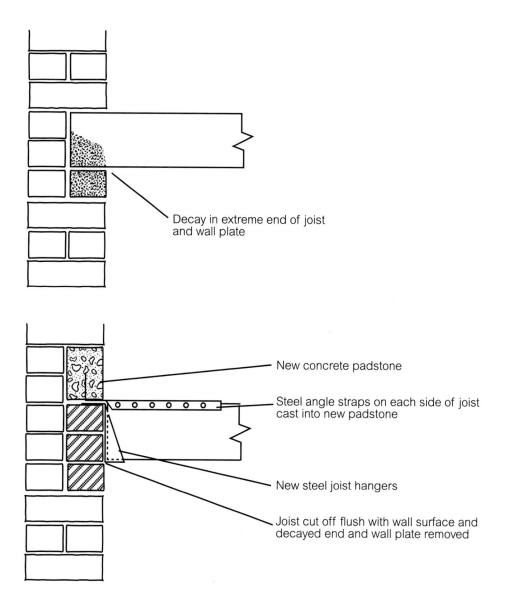

Decay in extreme end of joist and wall plate

New concrete padstone

Steel angle straps on each side of joist cast into new padstone

New steel joist hangers

Joist cut off flush with wall surface and decayed end and wall plate removed

Fig. 7.8 Mechanical repair of decayed joist ends using straps and joist hangers

cutting away the decay and using splice joints and through-bolts to mechanically connect the new timber to the sound, unaffected timber. The connection of the new truss end to the existing is completed by fixing steel through-bolted splice plates to each side of the splice joints. This technique is illustrated in Figs. 7.10–7.12.

Providing there is some residual strength in the roof truss end, despite the occurrence of decay, a simpler alternative to the above method is to treat the decayed timber with preservative and fix steel gusset plates on each side. The preservative-treated, weakened end of the truss is retained as a base for fixing through-bolted triangular steel gusset plates to each side. The gusset plates should extend beyond the decayed area, over-

lapping by at least 150mm with the sound, unaffected timber.

Figs. 7.13 and 7.14 illustrate this technique and Fig. 7.15 shows the use of nailed plywood gussets as an alternative to steel plate.

7.8 Epoxy resin-based repair and restoration of decayed structural timbers

An alternative method to mechanical techniques for the repair of decayed structural timbers, and one which has increased in popularity during the last 20 years, involves

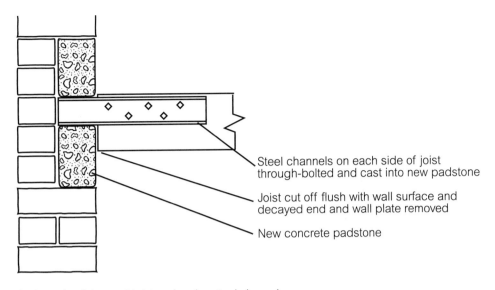

Fig. 7.9 Mechanical repair of decayed joist ends using steel channels

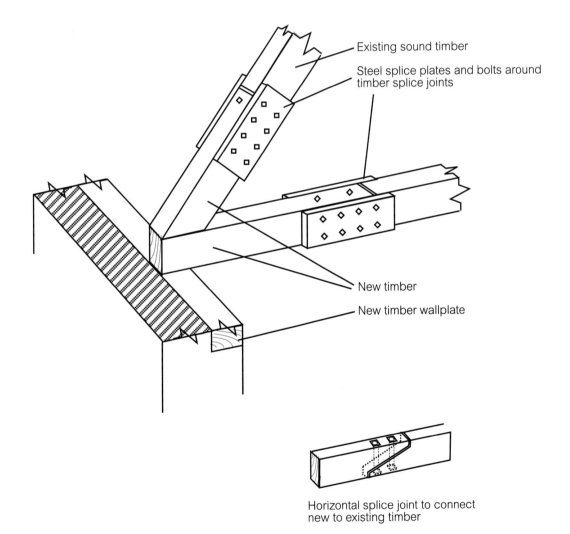

Horizontal splice joint to connect
new to existing timber

Fig. 7.10 Repair to decayed roof truss ends using replacement timber and steel splice plates

Fig. 7.11   Splice joint repair to decayed roof truss end

Fig. 7.12   Splice joint repair to decayed roof truss end showing through-bolted steel splice plates

the use of epoxy resin-based systems. The use of synthetic resins for the repair of damaged or defective concrete members had been common for many years prior to their more recent successful application to timber repair.

With timber restoration, the bonding capability of the synthetic resin is not the only criterion in effecting a successful repair: reinforcing rods of glass-fibre or polyester and steel reinforcing bars and plates also play a major role in the techniques employed. It is essential,

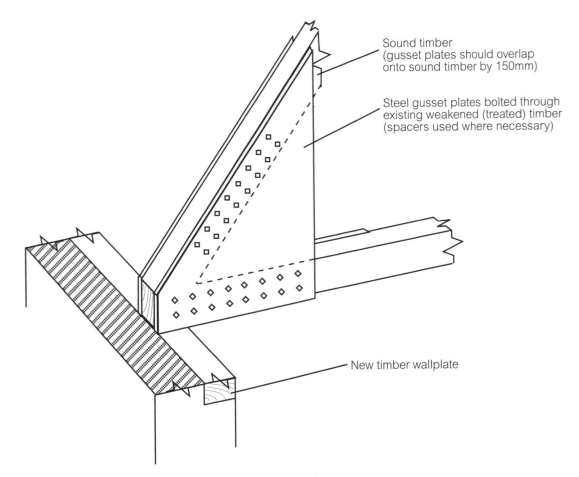

Sound timber
(gusset plates should overlap
onto sound timber by 150mm)

Steel gusset plates bolted through
existing weakened (treated) timber
(spacers used where necessary)

New timber wallplate

Fig. 7.13   Repair to decayed roof truss ends using steel gusset plates

Fig. 7.14   Steel gusset plate repair to decayed roof truss end

Fig. 7.15 Plywood gusset repair to decayed roof truss end

where reinforcement is used, that it is set deep into the sound portion of the timber to ensure an effective connection and load transfer, and the epoxy resins used must have good fluidity in order to obtain maximum penetration and impregnation of the wood fibres to obtain a good bond. Epoxy resin-based repair involves highly specialised skills, and the selection of resin mixes, reinforcement types and solutions to individual problems requires a thorough understanding of the techniques available. It is therefore essential, where it is considered that this type of repair and restoration might be appropriate in a particular refurbishment scheme, to call in one of the specialist contractors experienced in such work.

7.8.1 Repair of decayed joist and beam ends

In-situ, resin-based repair techniques are now widely used as an alternative to the traditional repair methods which involve splicing-in new timber and using steel plates, angles and bolts. A typical resin-based beam end repair

system is illustrated and described in Fig. 7.16 and a completed repair is shown in Fig. 7.17.

The work involves removing the decayed wood at the beam end and replacing it with a new epoxy-resin 'foot' which is bonded to the sound timber using polyester reinforcement rods embedded in epoxy resin.

7.8.2 Repair of decayed roof truss ends

An effective technique of carrying out structural restoration of decayed roof truss ends is described below, and illustrated in Fig. 7.18. Where a roof truss has decayed at the wall plate, a reinforcing plate is introduced into the main tie beam, and the decayed end timber cut out and replaced with epoxy-resin mortar. Additional corner reinforcement in the form of reinforcing bars can be inserted into holes drilled through the end of the rafter to pass each side of the reinforcing plate in the main tie beam. It is essential that the reinforcing plate and bars are set and fully bonded deep into the sound portion of the timber if a totally effective repair is to be achieved.

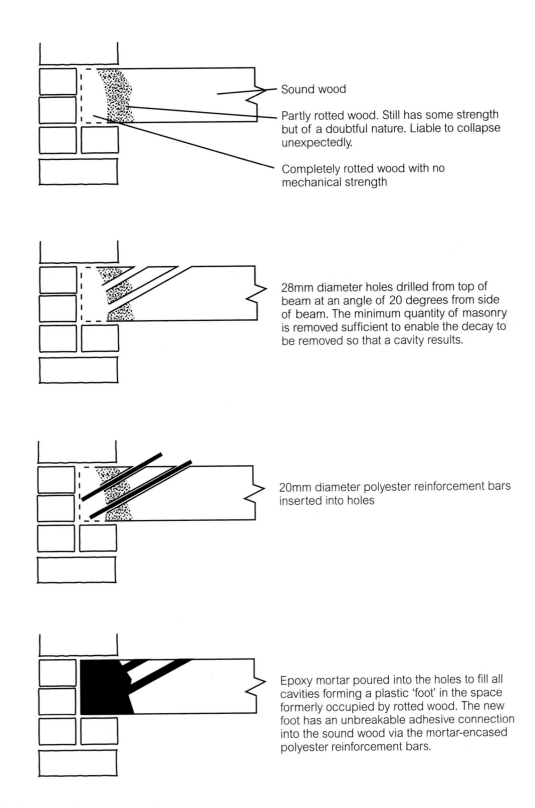

Sound wood

Partly rotted wood. Still has some strength but of a doubtful nature. Liable to collapse unexpectedly.

Completely rotted wood with no mechanical strength

28mm diameter holes drilled from top of beam at an angle of 20 degrees from side of beam. The minimum quantity of masonry is removed sufficient to enable the decay to be removed so that a cavity results.

20mm diameter polyester reinforcement bars inserted into holes

Epoxy mortar poured into the holes to fill all cavities forming a plastic 'foot' in the space formerly occupied by rotted wood. The new foot has an unbreakable adhesive connection into the sound wood via the mortar-encased polyester reinforcement bars.

Fig. 7.16 Resin-based beam end repair system

Fig. 7.17   Epoxy resin-based repair to decayed beam end

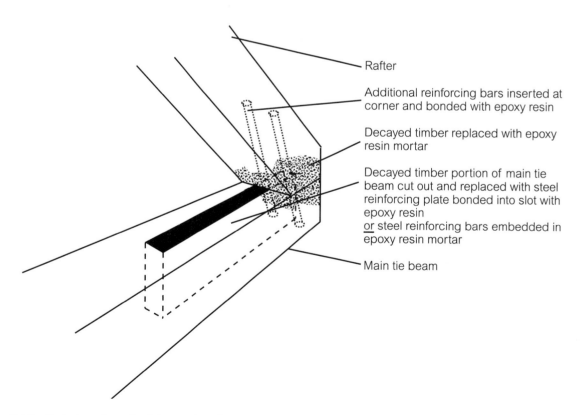

Rafter

Additional reinforcing bars inserted at corner and bonded with epoxy resin

Decayed timber replaced with epoxy resin mortar

Decayed timber portion of main tie beam cut out and replaced with steel reinforcing plate bonded into slot with epoxy resin
or steel reinforcing bars embedded in epoxy resin mortar

Main tie beam

Fig. 7.18   Resin-based repair of decayed roof truss ends

7.8.3 Repair of decayed beams between supports

In some buildings which have suffered from neglect over a lengthy period, timber decay may be more widespread, and not merely restricted to those more vulnerable areas discussed above. Timber decay may occur in beams, rafters and the main ties of roof trusses between their supports, and epoxy-resin repair techniques are effective enough to be capable of repairing structural timbers that have virtually completely rotted through. A repair technique employed for this purpose is illustrated in Fig. 7.19 and involves inserting steel bar or plate reinforcement into a specially cut slot which extends deeply into the sound timber of the beam on each side of the decayed area. The plate is fully bonded into the slot with epoxy resin, and epoxy-resin mortar is used to fill the void left after cutting out the area of decayed timber.

7.8.4 General repairs to decayed timber members

In addition to the repairs described above, epoxy resin-based repair techniques, using various types of reinforcement and epoxy-resin mortars, can also be used to effect permanent repairs to decayed timbers and joints in many other situations where fungal or insect attack has taken place. As stated previously, where this type of repair might be considered appropriate, a specialist contractor should be consulted in the first instance.

References

Building Research Establishment (1991) *Design of Timber Floors to Prevent Decay* (Digest 364), BRE, Watford.

Building Research Establishment (1993) *Wood Preservatives: Application Methods* (Digest 378), BRE, Watford.

Building Research Establishment (1996) *Reducing the Risk of Pest Infestation in Buildings* (Digest 415), BRE, Watford.

Building Research Establishment (1997) *Repairing Timber Windows: Parts 1 & 2* (Good Repair Guide 10), BRE, Watford.

Building Research Establishment (1997) *Wood Rot: Assessing and Treating Decay* (Good Repair Guide 12), BRE, Watford.

Building Research Establishment (1998) *Wood-boring Insect Attack: Identifying and Treating Damage: Parts 1 & 2* (Good Repair Guide 8), BRE, Watford.

Richardson, B.A. (1991) *Defects and Deterioration in Buildings*, E. & F.N. Spon, London.

Ridout, B. (1998) 'The Durability and Decay of Oak', *The Building Conservation Directory 1998*, ed. J. Taylor, Cathedral Communications Ltd., Tisbury, 97–9.

University of Bath, Department of Architecture and Building Engineering (1985) *Building Appraisal Maintenance and Preservation: Symposium Proceedings*, University of Bath.

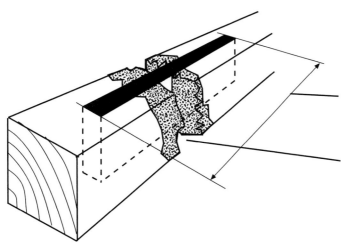

Slot cut in beam to allow insertion of steel reinforcing plate bonded into slot with epoxy resin or steel reinforcing bars embedded in epoxy resin mortar

Badly decayed section of beam at or near mid-span replaced with epoxy resin mortar

Fig. 7.19 Resin-based repair of decayed beams

8
Strengthening of existing timber floors

8.1 General

In certain refurbishment and alteration schemes, the existing floors may need to be strengthened in order to cater for increased loadings imposed by the proposed new use. The most common examples occur where existing buildings are converted to office use. In such cases the existing timber floors may not be capable of carrying the excessive localised loads imposed by modern filing and storage systems, office machinery and equipment.

A number of solutions are available where an existing timber floor needs to be strengthened, and the most common techniques are described below.

8.2 Replacing with new timber or steel sections

The existing floor beams are replaced with new timber or steel sections capable of supporting the increased loads. This solution usually involves major disruption to the existing structure and often necessitates removal and reinstatement of the existing floorboards, joists and ceiling. In view of the considerable expense and inconvenience involved, the method is not, therefore, generally recommended, and an alternative solution should be considered.

8.3 Strengthening with new steel channel sections

The existing floor beams are strengthened with new steel channel sections fixed to both sides to cater for the increased floor loadings. This technique is also very disruptive and expensive, requiring the removal of floorboards and ceilings, the cutting back of floor joists and reinstatement of their ends onto the new steel channels. Access holes may also need to be formed through the existing external walls to allow insertion of the steel channels.

8.4 Stiffening with steel or timber

The existing floor beams are stiffened with steel or timber fixed to their top or bottom surfaces. Fig. 8.1 shows the application of this solution using epoxy-resin bonding and dowelling techniques to increase the depth of a floor beam. The additional depth of timber may be built up in laminations, bonded to the existing and each other, using epoxy adhesive. Alternatively, a single piece of timber may be added and bonded to the existing beam using epoxy adhesive and reinforcing dowels set in epoxy-resin mortar.

Clearly, this solution will either raise the floor level, or lower the ceiling level, and it will also involve partial disruption of the existing floor or ceiling. In view of these factors, therefore, this method of floor strengthening may not be appropriate in certain circumstances.

8.5 Stiffening with steel plates

The existing floor beams are stiffened by means of steel plates fixed to both sides. Where supported members (for example, secondary beams and/or floor joists) are seated on top of the member being strengthened, this technique will produce an effective and economic

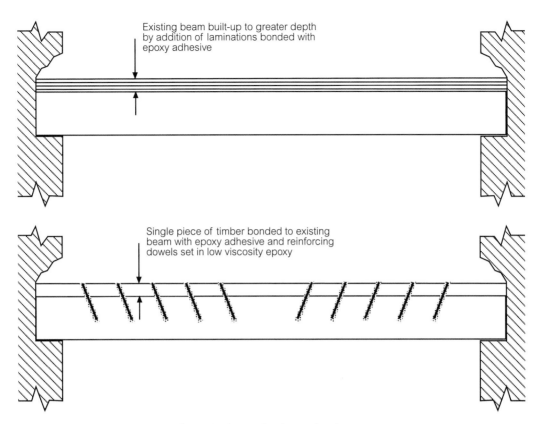

Fig. 8.1   Strengthening of existing timber floors by increasing beam depths

method of strengthening. However, where supported members are connected to the sides of the member being strengthened, the detailing and fixing can be cumbersome, time-consuming and expensive.

8.6 Strengthening with steel stiffening reinforcement

The existing floor beams are strengthened by inserting steel stiffening reinforcement, embedded in low-viscosity epoxy, within their thickness.

This technique, invented and developed by RTT Restoration Ltd., is illustrated in Fig. 8.2 and involves cutting a slot out of the centre of the beam and inserting a number of steel reinforcing bars embedded in, and bonded to the existing timber, with low-viscosity epoxy. The size of the slot, and the number and diameter of reinforcing bars, are designed to suit the particular circumstances, an increase of 50% in load-carrying capacity being possible in the majority of cases. The advantages of this technique over those previously described are:

- access is required only from above the beam
- disturbance of the existing floor is minimised
- disturbance of the existing ceiling is avoided, a particularly important advantage where the ceiling is ornate or has to be preserved as part of a listing requirement
- the existing components are fully retained
- any existing distortion can be accommodated, since the reinforcing bars can be bent to match the beam's deflected shape if necessary
- it avoids the need to form holes in existing walls to introduce replacement members
- it obviates the need to manhandle heavy materials or components
- it does not adversely affect the fire-resistance of the existing construction.

As an alternative to the use of steel reinforcing bars, as described above, steel plate may be inserted into the slot and embedded in low-viscosity epoxy as shown in Figs. 8.3–8.5.

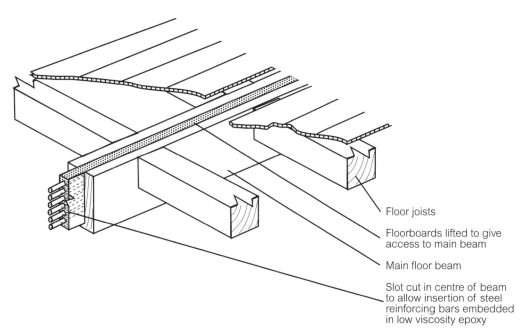

Floor joists

Floorboards lifted to give access to main beam

Main floor beam

Slot cut in centre of beam to allow insertion of steel reinforcing bars embedded in low viscosity epoxy

Fig. 8.2   Strengthening of existing timber floors by insertion of resin-bonded stiffening reinforcement

Fig. 8.3   Floor-beam strengthening using steel plate embedded in low-viscosity epoxy

Fig. 8.4 Floor-beam strengthening using steel plate embedded in low-viscosity epoxy

Fig. 8.5 Temporary support to beam during strengthening work

References

University of Bath, Department of Architecture and Building Engineering (1985) *Building Appraisal Maintenance and Preservation: Symposium Proceedings*, University of Bath.

9
Heavy-lifting systems

9.1 General

Occasionally, building refurbishment work necessitates the use of highly specialised skills and equipment to carry out major structural alterations which involve the large-scale movement or lifting of entire buildings or elements.

9.2 Movement of complete buildings

One of the most publicised recent examples of the movement of a complete building was the moving of the Belle Tout lighthouse at Beachy Head, East Sussex, in early 1999. Continuous erosion of the chalk cliffs had left the 850-tonne granite lighthouse within 5 metres of the cliff-edge, having originally been built some 30 metres back from the edge. To save the lighthouse, which had been converted some years earlier to a dwelling, the entire structure was jacked up and 'slid' 17 metres further inland, away from the cliff-edge, onto a newly constructed foundation using specialist computerised sliding equipment. This involved providing a cradle of new reinforced concrete beams beneath the structure, jacking the whole building up by 600mm using 22 hydraulic jacks, and then using 6 hydraulic rams to push the structure 17 metres, along 4 concrete tracks, before lowering it down onto its new foundation.

This project was carried out by Abbey Pynford, a company specialising in the movement of complete buildings and other heavy-lifting/movement applications.

9.3 Movement of building elements

Heavy-lifting technology of the type described above can also be applied to the movement of structural elements of buildings to facilitate their refurbishment and re-use. One such project, also carried out by Abbey Pynford, involved raising the height of the complete roof structure of the Granary Building, a Grade II* listed canalside warehouse in Leeds.

The Granary Building, shown in Figure 9.5, was built c.1778 for the Leeds and Liverpool Canal Company as the canal's eastern terminus warehouse at its junction with the River Aire near to Leeds city centre. The building is four storeys high, built of coursed, squared stone with a graduated stone slate roof. The canal channel extended into the building, as shown in Figs. 9.1 and 9.3, to enable boats to be loaded and unloaded inside. The massive timber roof structure comprises cross-beams supporting queen posts clasping a collar, x-braces and six rows of purlins. The interior was remodelled in the mid to late nineteenth century to give a safer, fire-proof construction, the original timber floors being replaced by concrete vaults supported on two rows of cast-iron columns. Other additions at this time included a gantry and slate roof canopy and a lower extension block at the western end of the building (see Fig. 9.2).

By the early 1990s the building, which had been empty and neglected for a long period, had fallen into a state of disrepair but was given a new lease of life in 1995 through its restoration and refurbishment to produce modern office accommodation. The existing structure, including the roof and concrete vaulted floors, was still structurally sound and therefore completely retained. The original canal channel, inside the building, was drained and

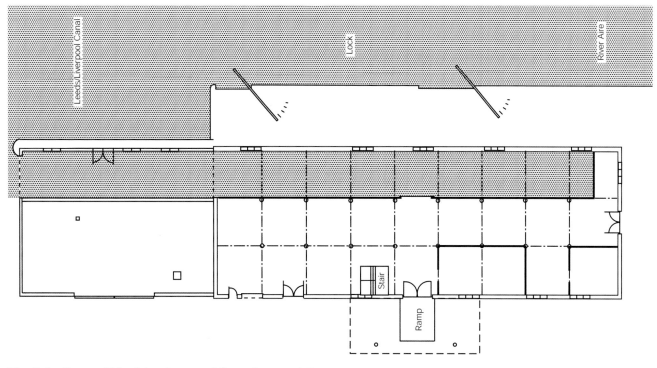

Fig. 9.1 Granary Wharf, Leeds: ground-floor plan as existing

Fig. 9.2 Granary Wharf, Leeds: south elevation as existing

covered with a new floor slab, and new raised floors provided over the existing floors to accommodate services. This enabled the existing vaulted floor soffits to remain exposed as a feature in the new design.

A major design problem with the Granary Building was that the fourth storey did not provide sufficient clear headroom beneath the existing exposed queen-post roof structure to enable its use as office space, meaning that 25% of the building's potential floor area was effectively unusable (see Figs. 9.3 and 9.5). However, in view of the building's prime location in a rapidly growing and attractive commercial area, the developer decided that it would be feasible to incur the significant cost of physically raising the existing roof height, using specialist heavy-lifting technology, to enable the fourth storey to be converted into office accommodation (see Fig. 9.4). The existing clear headroom of 2.1 metres beneath the existing roof structure had to be increased by 300mm to 2.4 metres to enable the upper storey to be converted into office space (see Fig. 9.4) and this was achieved using a specialised hydraulically operated and computer-monitored jacking system provided by Abbey Pynford.

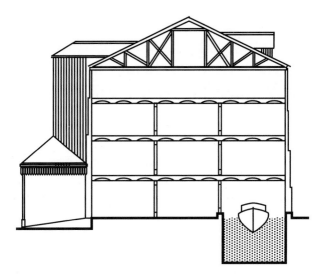

Fig. 9.3 Granary Wharf, Leeds: cross-section as existing

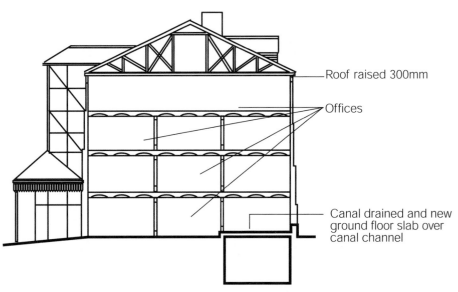

Roof raised 300mm

Offices

Canal drained and new
ground floor slab over
canal channel

Fig. 9.4 Granary Wharf, Leeds: cross-section as proposed

The sequence of operations in lifting the roof of the Granary Building was as follows:

- Stone-slate roof covering removed to reduce loading on roof structure.
- Temporary weatherproof sheeting applied over roof.
- Temporary steelwork supports to tops of walls installed internally and externally immediately below roof level to prevent walls spreading outwards during the works. The internal components of these supports are shown in Figs. 9.6, 9.7 and 9.8.
- Temporary steel jacking infrastructure installed

with jacks located under ends of each queen-post truss (see Fig. 9.6).

- Stonework removed from ends of roof trusses to 'free' the trusses prior to jacking.
- Hydraulic jacks connected to central console and all trusses simultaneously jacked up by 300mm (see Fig. 9.7).
- New supporting padstones inserted under ends of roof trusses (see Fig. 9.8).
- New stonework built up around padstones and roof truss ends (see Fig. 9.9).
- New roof insulation installed and slate battens laid.
- Stone-slate roof covering replaced.

Fig. 9.5 The Granary Building, Leeds: north and east elevations

Fig. 9.6 The Granary Building, Leeds: temporary supports and jacks prior to lifting of roof

Fig. 9.7   The Granary Building, Leeds: after lifting of roof

Fig. 9.8   The Granary Building, Leeds: after lifting of roof showing new padstones inserted to support roof trusses

Fig. 9.9 The Granary Building, Leeds: after lifting of roof showing new padstone and new infill stonework

10
Underpinning systems

10.1 General

The purpose of underpinning is to take the level of an existing foundation to a deeper, firmer stratum by adding a new foundation construction beneath it, and this may be necessary for a range of different reasons, the most common of which are:

- Where excessive settlement of the existing foundation has occurred and has caused, or threatened, structural damage to the building.
- To permit the level of the adjacent ground to be lowered, for example for the construction of a new, adjacent building with a basement extending deeper than the existing foundations.
- To increase the loadbearing capacity of the existing foundation, for example because of increased floor loadings or the construction of an additional storey.

10.2 Precautions prior to and during underpinning

The operation of underpinning inevitably involves excavating beneath the existing foundation in order to construct the new foundation beneath it, and this temporarily puts the stability of the existing structure at risk. It is essential, therefore, that the following precautions are taken to minimise any risk caused by the underpinning excavations:

- Existing loads on the structure should be reduced by temporary removal of the building's contents where possible, especially where they are imposing excessive loading.

- Where the existing structure is weak, additional temporary works should be carried out to stabilise the existing building, such as raking shores to the walls being underpinned, internal flying shores and dead shoring.
- During the underpinning works, a constant check should be kept for any movement of the existing structure, using calibrated tell-tales, heavy plumb-bobs or laser monitoring devices.

10.3 Underpinning techniques

Techniques used for underpinning range from traditional methods, using brickwork or mass concrete, to more sophisticated methods involving needling and piling. The following sections describe some of the underpinning systems currently in use.

Generally, traditional brickwork and mass concrete underpinning can be carried out by the builder or general contractor, whilst the more sophisticated methods, especially those involving piling, are carried out by specialist sub-contractors such as Roger Bullivant, which offer complete survey, design and construction packages.

It should be noted that it is rarely necessary to underpin the whole of a building, since most settlement and subsidence problems are due to failure of only part of the existing foundation.

10.3.1 Brickwork underpinning

Brickwork underpinning is the most traditional of all of the techniques used and has largely been replaced by other methods. However, it is still useful for small underpinning works to brick and masonry structures.

The construction of brickwork underpinning, and its sequence of operations, is similar in all respects to mass concrete underpinning described in Section 10.3.2. A vertical cross-section of brickwork underpinning is shown in Fig. 10.1.

10.3.2 Mass concrete underpinning

Mass concrete underpinning is one of the most commonly used methods for both small and large buildings. The key factors in the design and construction of mass concrete underpinning are identified as follows (and illustrated in Fig. 10.2):

- The underpinning must be carried out in 'legs' in order to leave the greater proportion of the existing foundation fully supported throughout the operations.
- The maximum length of each leg depends on the stability of the existing structure, its loadings, and the subsoil conditions, and is generally between 0.9 and 1.5 metres.
- The total length of the unsupported legs of the existing foundation at any one time during the underpinning operations should not generally exceed one-sixth of its total length for unstable structures carrying heavy loads; one-quarter of its total length for larger buildings with good structural stability; one-third of its total length for small buildings with good structural stability.
- When one set of legs is completed and providing full support, the next set of legs is constructed. New legs should not be constructed immediately adjacent to legs which have just been completed.
- Each leg of mass concrete must be properly keyed to the next leg by using a 'joggle' joint or by hacking/scabbling the previous leg prior to casting the next.
- The mass concrete underpinning is constructed to within 75mm of the underside of the existing foundation and, on achieving its required strength, is 'pinned up'. This involves ramming a dry-mix concrete, comprising one part cement to one part fine aggregate, of maximum particle size 10mm, into the 75mm space. The purpose of this is to enable the mass concrete to undergo its initial, and most significant, drying shrinkage prior to achieving a positive structural connection between the existing foundation and its underpinning. Failure to carry out this operation would result in undesirable minor settlement of the underpinned foundation.

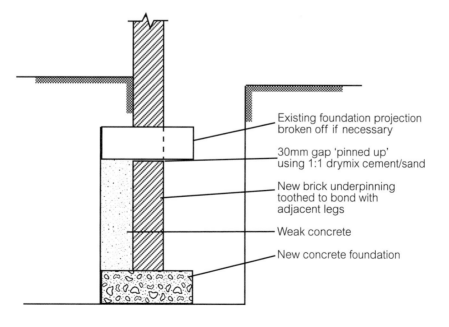

Existing foundation projection broken off if necessary

30mm gap 'pinned up' using 1:1 drymix cement/sand

New brick underpinning toothed to bond with adjacent legs

Weak concrete

New concrete foundation

Fig. 10.1 Brickwork underpinning

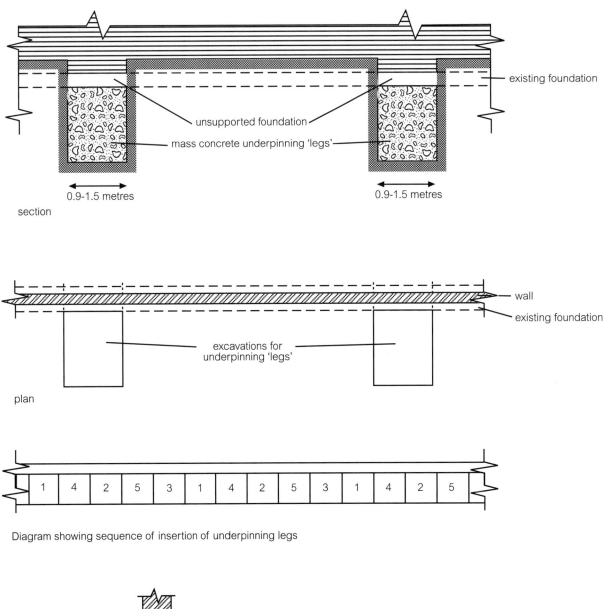

section

plan

Diagram showing sequence of insertion of underpinning legs

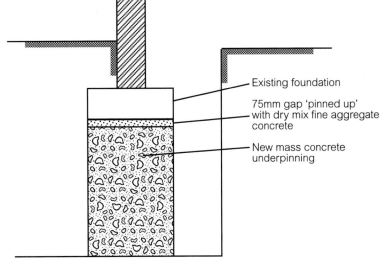

Fig. 10.2 Mass concrete underpinning

10.3.3 Beam and pier underpinning

Beam and pier underpinning, illustrated in Fig. 10.3, comprises a reinforced concrete beam, inserted either directly above or below the existing foundation, supported by mass concrete piers constructed at 2.5 to 3.0 metre centres. The function of the reinforced concrete beam is to transfer the loads from the wall being underpinned to the piers which, in turn, carry the loads to a deeper, firmer stratum.

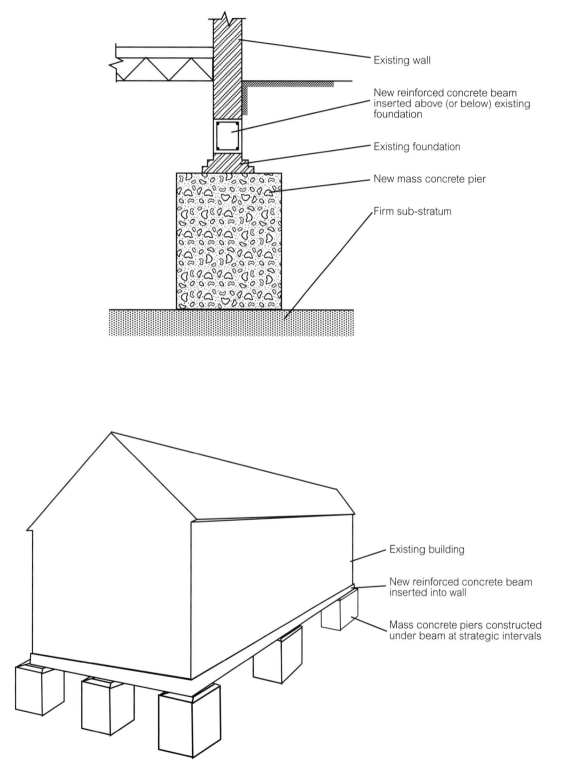

Existing wall

New reinforced concrete beam inserted above (or below) existing foundation

Existing foundation

New mass concrete pier

Firm sub-stratum

Existing building

New reinforced concrete beam inserted into wall

Mass concrete piers constructed under beam at strategic intervals

Fig. 10.3 Beam and pier underpinning

The sequence of operations is as follows:

- Excavation for mass concrete piers. The relatively small plan area of each pier is such that only a limited length of the existing foundation is undermined, therefore maintaining the stability of the structure.
- Construction of mass concrete piers to underside of existing foundation.
- Removal of masonry above existing foundation between piers for construction of reinforced concrete beam.
- Construction of reinforced concrete beam between piers.

As with traditional underpinning techniques, it is essential that the total length of unsupported/undermined existing structure at any one time is kept to a minimum. This is achieved by ensuring that the maximum total unsupported length does not exceed the recommendations given in Section 10.3.2. In certain cases, this may involve constructing the reinforced concrete beam between piers in stages, although for smaller buildings with good structural stability, this should not be necessary.

The principal advantage of beam and pier underpinning, compared with a traditional underpinning system, is that excavation beneath the existing structure is reduced from the entire length of wall to the piers only, thereby reducing the risk to the building's stability during the works.

10.3.4 Pile and needle underpinning

Pile and needle underpinning, illustrated in Fig. 10.4, comprises reinforced concrete needles inserted through the existing wall, above foundation level, and supported at each end by small diameter piles which transmit the building's loads to a deeper, firmer stratum. The needles are inserted at approximately 1.5 metre centres along the length of the wall being underpinned, their function being to transmit loading from the wall to the piles.

The actual needle centres and pile diameters and depths will be determined by the stability of the building, the loads to be transmitted and the subsoil conditions. The 100–250mm diameter piles are driven or bored using compact piling rigs which require only 1.80 metres

headroom and 2 x 1.5 metres working space, especially important when installing piles inside the building where space may be limited.

The principal advantage of the pile and needle system is that there is no direct undermining of the existing foundation, and only small areas of masonry need to be removed to construct the needles. This method is also faster than traditional systems involving bulk excavation. It should be borne in mind that pile and needle underpinning involves inserting piles from inside, as well as outside, the building which may cause disturbance to the occupants and day-to-day functioning of the building throughout the works. This, however, can be overcome by using pile and cantilever needle underpinning where the needles, supported by two piles installed outside the building, function as cantilevers, ruling out the need for any internal work. This method is illustrated in Fig. 10.5.

10.3.5 Cantilever ring beam underpinning

Cantilever ring beam underpinning, illustrated in Fig. 10.6, comprises steel 'I'-section cantilever needles which transmit the loads from the wall to a deeper bearing stratum by means of a reinforced concrete ring beam and mini-piles.

Two staggered lines of mini-piles, 90–250mm in diameter, are first driven, drilled or augered at approximately 1 metre centres alongside the wall being underpinned. The inner line of piles gives direct support to steel 'I'-section needles, and the outer line supports the reinforced concrete ring beam between the needles.

Following construction of the mini-piles, the steel needles are positioned, their inner ends located in pockets formed in the masonry, and the reinforced concrete ring beam is cast. The ring beam encases the needles and is connected to the tops of the piles to produce a fully integrated support.

The system is designed so that the loads from the underpinned wall place the inner line of piles in compression and the outer line of piles in tension. This method, by providing a direct connection between the needles and ring beam, gives continuous support to the wall along its entire length, rather than at intervals as with pile and needle underpinning (Section 10.3.4). It is therefore better suited to less stable walls in a more serious state of structural distress.

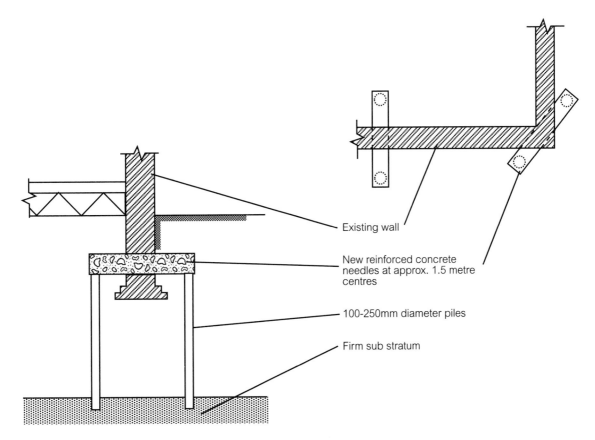

Fig. 10.4   Pile and needle underpinning

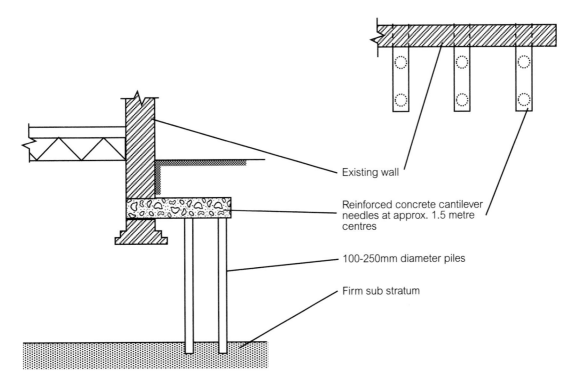

Fig. 10.5   Pile and cantilever needle underpinning

The principal advantages of cantilever ring beam underpinning are similar to those for pile and cantilever needle underpinning: no direct undermining of the existing foundation is necessary, only small areas of masonry need be removed for insertion of the needles, no bulk excavation is required, and all of the work can be executed from outside the building. The system is also faster than traditional 'dig-out' underpinning methods.

10.3.6 Double angle mini-pile underpinning

The double angle mini-pile underpinning system, illustrated in Fig. 10.7, involves the installation of small-diameter piles in pairs formed at an angle *through* the existing foundation at between 1.0 metre and 1.5 metre intervals.

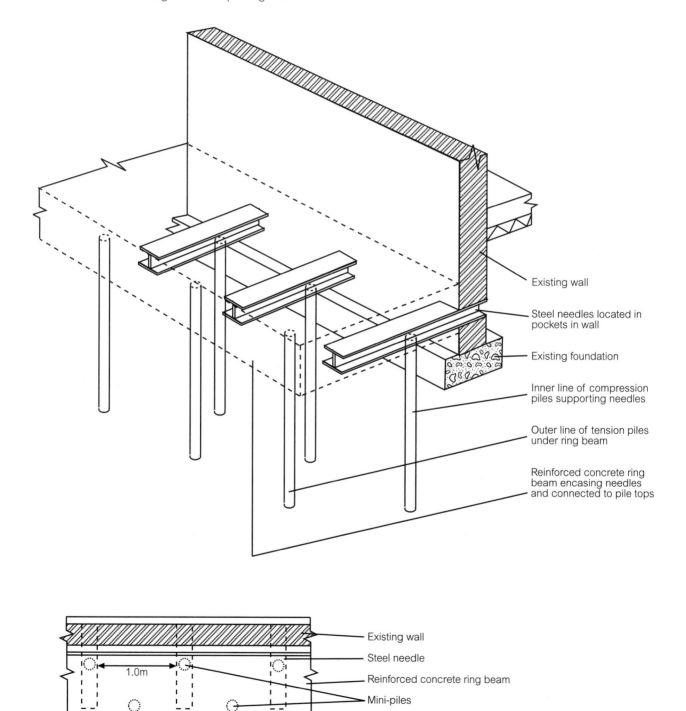

Existing wall

Steel needles located in pockets in wall

Existing foundation

Inner line of compression piles supporting needles

Outer line of tension piles under ring beam

Reinforced concrete ring beam encasing needles and connected to pile tops

Existing wall

Steel needle

Reinforced concrete ring beam

Mini-piles

1.0m

Fig. 10.6 Cantilever ring beam underpinning

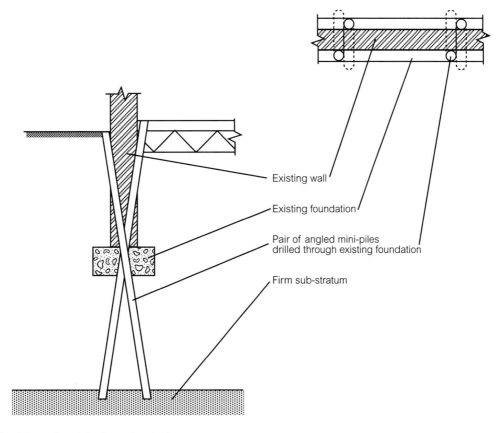

Existing wall

Existing foundation

Pair of angled mini-piles
drilled through existing foundation

Firm sub-stratum

Fig. 10.7   Double angle mini-pile underpinning

The existing foundation is pre-drilled using air-flushed rotary percussive equipment with drilling heads capable of drilling through brickwork, masonry, concrete and steel as necessary. Permanently cased steel-driven or solid- or hollow-stem augered piles are then installed through the pre-drilled holes with the casings terminated at the underside of the existing foundation. The piles are then concreted and reinforced up through the existing foundation. Double angle mini-pile underpinning involves less excavation and disruption than most of the alternative methods. Undermining of the existing foundation is negligible, especially when compared with traditional 'dig-out' techniques. In addition, the construction of the piles through the existing foundation achieves a more direct physical connection between the existing structure and the new underpinning. Other advantages of this system are its speed of installation and its high load capability, achieved using piles from 90mm to 250mm diameter penetrating to any reasonable depth.

In cases where access to the interior of the building for pile construction is a problem, single piles may be installed from the outside only at closer intervals of between 0.9 metres and 1.2 metres.

All of the underpinning systems described in Sections 10.3.3.–10.3.6, together with other underpinning and foundation stabilisation systems, are carried out as full survey, design and construct packages by Roger Bullivant, one of the UK's leading specialist foundation and underpinning engineers.

References

Building Research Establishment (1990) *Underpinning* (Digest 352), BRE, Watford.

Bullivant, R.A. (1996) *Underpinning: A Practical Guide*, Blackwell Science, Oxford.

Hunt, R., Dyer, R.H. and Driscoll, R. (1991) *Foundation Movement and Remedial Underpinning in Low Rise Buildings*, Building Research Establishment, Watford.

University of Bath, Department of Architecture and Building Engineering (1985) *Building Appraisal Maintenance and Preservation: Symposium Proceedings*, University of Bath.

11
Facade retention

11.1 General

As discussed in Section 1, refurbishment of a building normally involves keeping most of the existing structure and fabric and restoring, repairing and upgrading it to provide accommodation which meets current standards in terms of comfort, amenity and, in most cases, building legislation. This enables owners and developers to re-use what otherwise might be considered as obsolete, redundant or outdated buildings.

A more extreme form of building re-use, which keeps considerably less of the existing structure and fabric than 'low-key' refurbishment, involves retaining only the external facade and constructing an entirely new structure behind it. Facade retention, as it has become known, may involve retaining only one elevation if the building is part of a 'row' of buildings forming a street frontage; two elevations if it is a corner building; three elevations if it forms the end of a block; or, more rarely, all four elevations if it is an isolated building. Whichever of the above a facade retention scheme may be, the entire interior and roof are normally demolished leaving only the external wall(s) standing to form the preserved external elevation(s) to a completely new structure erected behind.

The retention of existing facades in this way, in what might be regarded as the most drastic form of building refurbishment/re-use, short of total demolition, has become increasingly common during the last 25 years and requires special solutions to the technological problems that it presents. The principal problems met with all facade retention schemes include providing temporary support to the facade throughout the works; permanently tying back the facade to the new structure

erected behind it; allowing for differential settlement between the new structure and the retained facade; and ensuring that the new structure's foundations do not impair the stability of the retained facade.

11.2 Temporary support systems

In all buildings comprising loadbearing external facade walls, there is an interdependency between those walls and the elements they carry. Whilst the external facade walls provide structural support to many internal elements (floors, roof structure and some cross-walls), these internal elements, in turn, provide lateral support to the facade. Thus, when this lateral support to the facade is totally removed by demolishing the building's interior, it becomes necessary to provide some means of temporary support to the facade until the new structure is constructed and the retained facade tied back to it. A major consideration in the design of a temporary support system is that it must provide the facade with stability and resistance against wind-loads from both sides, to which it will be subjected for an extensive period during the works whilst the building is opened up to the elements.

Generally, temporary support systems to retained facades fall into three categories: wholly external, located entirely outside the facade; wholly internal, located behind the facade within the zone of the existing and new structures; or part internal/part external, some of the supporting elements being located behind, and some outside, the facade.

External support systems have the important advantages of not interfering with demolition or subsequent construction work, but they often obstruct adjacent footpaths and roadways, and, in many schemes, have not been permitted for that reason. Internal support systems, on the other hand, leave adjacent thoroughfares unobstructed but place severe constraints upon the progress and efficiency of both the demolition of the existing structure and the new construction work. Part internal/part external systems combine the advantages and disadvantages of both.

It is essential, whatever category of temporary support system is used, that it is installed, and capable of giving total support to the facade, before any demolition of the building's internal structure takes place, and that it remains in position until the facade is permanently tied back to the newly erected structure behind. It is clear, therefore, that if an internal support system is used, its design will be complicated by having to ensure that it does not conflict either with elements of the existing building or of the new building. In addition, some members of the internal support system will inevitably interfere with the demolition operations and erection of the new structure. In certain cases, the nature of the scheme may require that the temporary support system is partly internal and partly external. The main difficulty with a part internal/part external support system is that it combines the disadvantages of both: adjacent footpaths, and possibly roadways, may be obstructed by the external elements, and demolition and construction operations are interfered with by the internal elements.

Figs. 11.1 and 11.2 show a typical tubular scaffolding external support system used on a scheme at East Parade, Leeds. The independent tied scaffold, erected off a steel gantry to allow the pavement to remain open, acted as a vertical cantilever to which the facade was tied by means of horizontal and vertical scaffold tubing, timber wall plates and folding wedges (see detail in Fig. 11.1).

Figs. 11.3, 11.4 and 11.5 show the use of the new structure's new steel frame as a wholly internal 'temporary' support system on a scheme at Colmore Row, Birmingham. This is a fairly common method of providing internal support to a facade during a project and has the advantage of utilising part of the new structure, rather than a wholly temporary support system, to hold up the facade. The first bay of the new steel frame is erected by 'threading' it through openings made in the existing structure before demolition takes place. The facade is then tied back to the frame (see detail in Fig. 11.3, and

Fig. 11.5), following which demolition can take place. The remainder of the new steel frame is then erected.

Fig. 11.6 shows an RMD proprietary external facade support system which uses standard 'slimshor' components. The principal advantage of the RMD system, in comparison with the alternatives, is that it uses far fewer components and is much quicker to erect and dismantle. RMD Ltd. also provide a full survey, design and erection service. Fig. 11.7 shows an RMD system in use on a facade retention scheme at Clumber Street, Nottingham.

Figs. 11.8 and 11.11 show a wholly internal temporary support system used at St Paul's House, Park Square, Leeds. The local authority would not permit any encroachment onto the narrow footpaths and streets on three sides of the retained facade and the contractor, therefore, had no choice but to design an internal temporary support system. This comprised four structural steel 'military trestle' towers in the centre of the building which supported tubular steel box-section flying shores at two levels. A combination of twin timber walings, folding wedges and steel through-bolts at the outer ends of the flying shores provided a supporting 'collar' to the facade throughout the project (see Fig. 11.8). As previously stated, such a system places severe constraints on both the demolition and new construction works since the temporary supports must be erected prior to commencement of the demolition, and remain in place until the new structure is complete and the facade tied back to it.

11.3 Facade ties

A problem common to all facade retention schemes involves permanently tying back the retained facade to the new structure erected behind it. The lateral support formerly provided by the original internal structure must be replaced by some form of mechanical tie system between the facade and the new structure. These facade ties must fulfil a number of important functional requirements:

● They must effectively hold back the retained facade and prevent any outward movement away from the new structure.

● They must not transmit any vertical loads from the new structure to the facade (since the facade

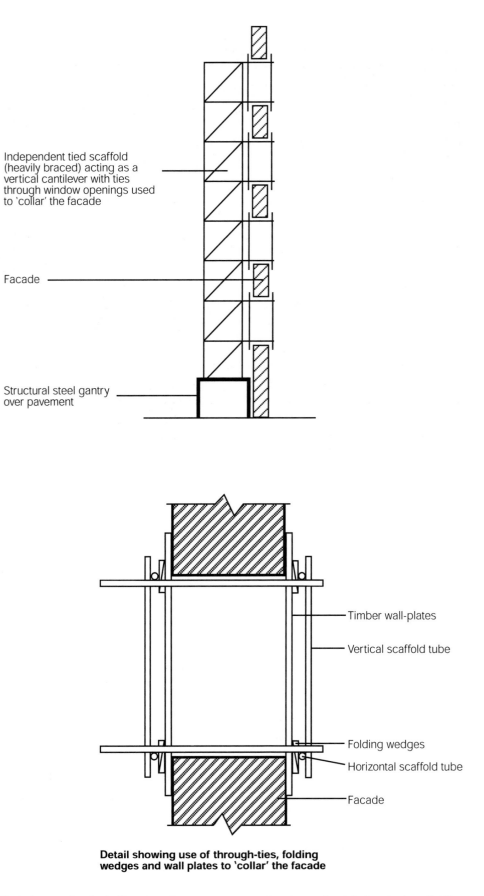

Independent tied scaffold
(heavily braced) acting as a
vertical cantilever with ties
through window openings used
to 'collar' the facade

Facade

Structural steel gantry
over pavement

Timber wall-plates

Vertical scaffold tube

Folding wedges

Horizontal scaffold tube

Facade

**Detail showing use of through-ties, folding
wedges and wall plates to 'collar' the facade**

Fig. 11.1 Typical example of wholly external temporary support system using tubular steel scaffolding components

Fig. 11.2 Tubular scaffolding external facade support system, East Parade, Leeds

should not normally act as a loadbearing element in the new design).

- They must be capable of accommodating any predicted differential settlement between the new structure and the retained facade without causing damage to the ties themselves, the facade or the new structure (see Section 11.4).

The most widely used solution to this problem is to employ some form of resin anchor system which involves anchoring steel tie-bars into the facade masonry with a rapid-setting resinous mortar and then connecting them directly or indirectly to the new structure. The anchoring of the tie-bars into the facade masonry may be executed using either a resin cartridge or pre-mixed resin. With the resin cartridge method, a pre-formed plastic or glass phial, containing the unmixed ingredients capable of forming the rapid-setting resinous mortar, is inserted into a pre-drilled hole in the masonry. The tie-bar is then spun into the hole using a drilling tool, breaking the cartridge and mixing its ingredients to form the mortar which

anchors the bar firmly into the masonry. The alternative method is to pump pre-mixed resinous mortar into a pre-drilled hole and either spin or push the tie-bar into it. The resin-anchoring procedure is illustrated in Fig. 11.9.

The connections between the projecting tie-bars and the new structure can be effected in a number of ways (Fig. 11.10). Methods used include casting the projecting tie-bars directly into the edges of the new floor slabs, or by using indirect connections where steel angles, bolted to the edges of the new structure, are fastened to the projecting resin-anchored tie-bars using locknuts. Fig. 11.11 (bottom left-hand corner) shows a typical indirect steel angle facade-tie system used on a scheme at St Paul's House, Leeds.

As an alternative to using resin-anchored tie-bars, various forms of through-tie may be used. These comprise steel bars passing completely through the facade, and secured to steel plates on the external face. The inner ends of the tie-bars project from the internal face of the facade and are secured to the new structure directly or indirectly in the same way as resin-anchored

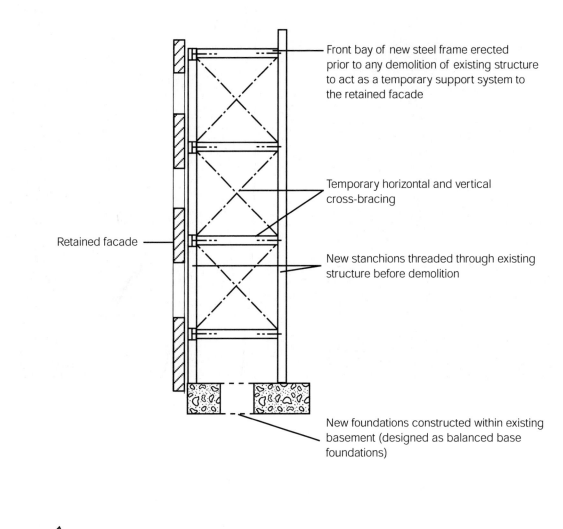

Front bay of new steel frame erected prior to any demolition of existing structure to act as a temporary support system to the retained facade

Temporary horizontal and vertical cross-bracing

Retained facade

New stanchions threaded through existing structure before demolition

New foundations constructed within existing basement (designed as balanced base foundations)

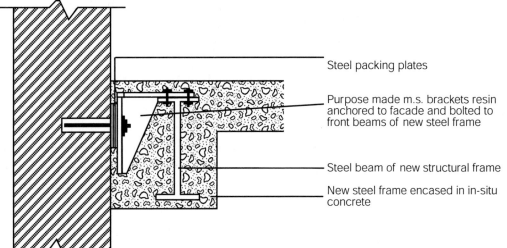

Steel packing plates

Purpose made m.s. brackets resin anchored to facade and bolted to front beams of new steel frame

Steel beam of new structural frame

New steel frame encased in in-situ concrete

Detail showing connection between steel frame and facade

Fig. 11.3 Internal facade support system employing part of new steel frame

Fig. 11.4 Wholly internal facade support system, Colmore Row, Birmingham, showing use of new steel frame to provide support

Fig. 11.5 Wholly internal facade support system, Colmore Row, Birmingham, showing resin-anchor ties used to tie back facade to new steel frame

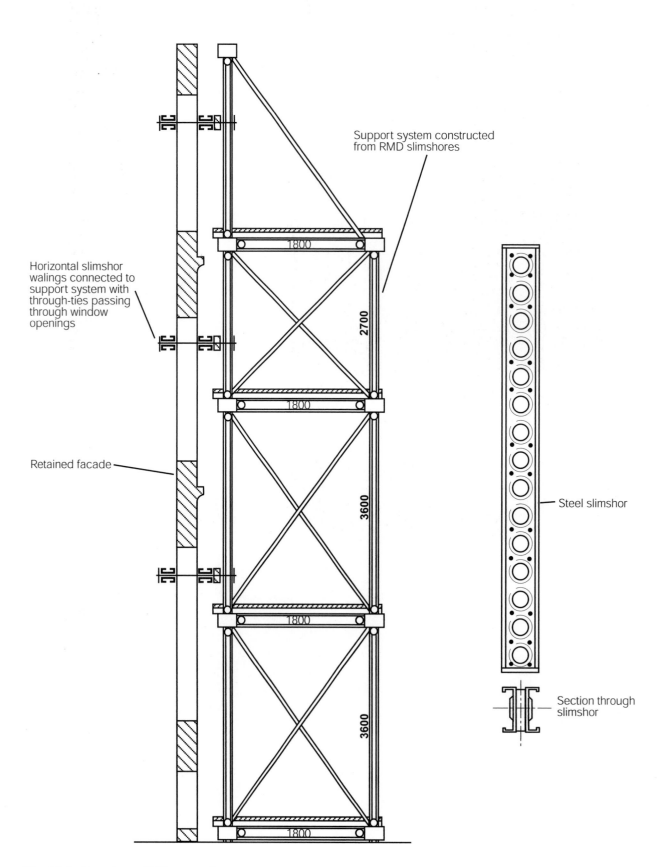

Support system constructed from RMD slimshores

Horizontal slimshor walings connected to support system with through-ties passing through window openings

Retained facade

1800

2700

1800

3600

1800

3600

1800

Steel slimshor

Section through slimshor

Fig. 11.6 Proprietary RMD external support system

Fig. 11.7 RMD external facade support system, Clumber Street, Nottingham

tie-bars. One problem with this through-tie method involves the concealment of the outer ends of the tie-bars and anchor plates, which is relatively easy with stuccoed or rendered facades, but more difficult with masonry or brickwork.

11.4 Differential settlement

It is essential in facade retention schemes that the detailing at the junction of the new structure and existing facade allows settlement of the former to occur if this has been predicted. A rigid connection between the new structure and the facade could result in potentially serious structural damage in the event of settlement. If such settlement has been predicted, its extent should be calculated using data from the subsoil investigations. The facade-ties and interface detail between the facade and the new structure should then be designed to allow this settlement to take place without causing damage to either of the structures or the facade-ties themselves. One of the most effective ways of achieving this is to use an indirect steel angle tie with a vertical slotted hole through which the resin-anchored tie-bar passes, as shown in Fig. 11.12. The slotted hole in the vertical leg of the angle enables the new structure to settle without causing damage.

The interface treatment between the new structure and the retained facade must also be considered where settlement of the former has been predicted. The interface between the new structure and the retained facade is usually at the outer faces of the new structure's

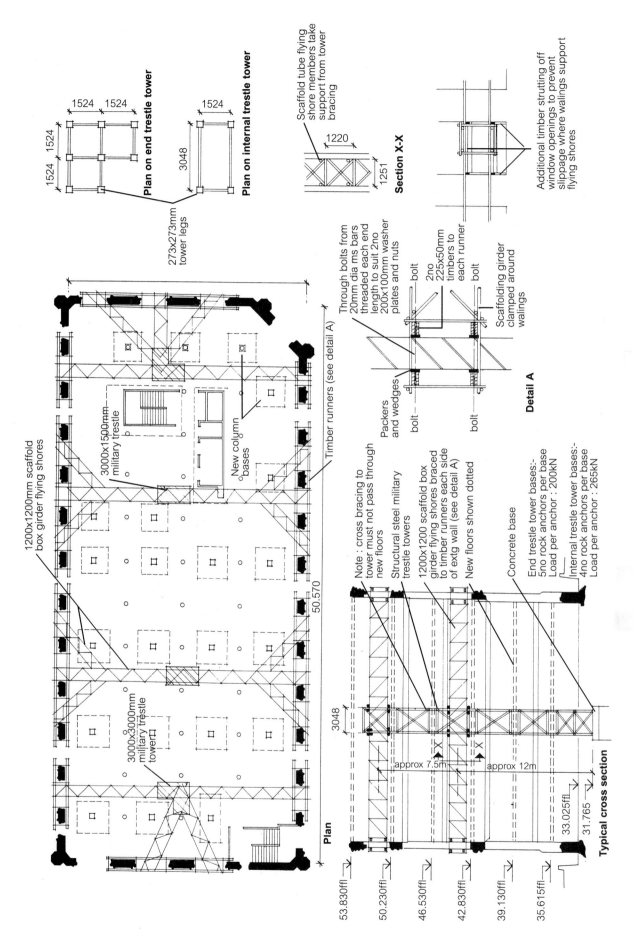

Plan on end trestle tower

1524 1524 1524

1524

1524

Plan on internal trestle tower

1524

3048

273x273mm tower legs

Scaffold tube flying shore members take support from tower bracing

1220

1251

Section X-X

Additional timber strutting off window openings to prevent slippage where walings support flying shores

Through bolts from 20mm dia ms bars threaded each end length to suit 2no 200x100mm washer plates and nuts

2no 225x50mm timbers to each runner

bolt

bolt

Scaffolding girder clamped around walings

Packers and wedges

bolt

bolt

Detail A

1200x1200mm scaffold box girder flying shores

3000x1500mm military trestle

New column bases

Timber runners (see detail A)

3000x3000mm military trestle tower

50.570

Plan

Note : cross bracing to tower must not pass through new floors

Structural steel military trestle towers

1200x1200 scaffold box girder flying shores braced to timber runners each side of extg wall (see detail A)

New floors shown dotted

Concrete base

End trestle tower bases:- 5no rock anchors per base Load per anchor : 200kN

Internal trestle tower bases:- 4no rock anchors per base Load per anchor : 265kN

3048

approx 7.5m   approx 12m

53.830ffl

50.230ffl

46.530ffl

42.830ffl

39.130ffl

35.615ffl

33.025ffl

31.765

Typical cross section

Fig. 11.8 Internal facade support system employing structural steelwork towers and tubular steel scaffolding components

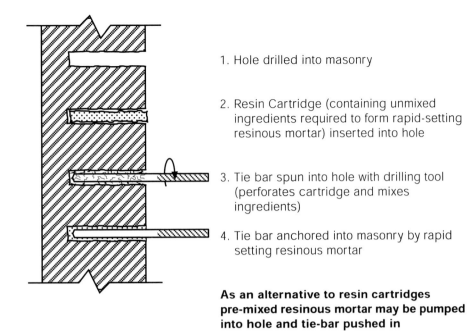

1. Hole drilled into masonry

2. Resin Cartridge (containing unmixed ingredients required to form rapid-setting resinous mortar) inserted into hole

3. Tie bar spun into hole with drilling tool (perforates cartridge and mixes ingredients)

4. Tie bar anchored into masonry by rapid setting resinous mortar

As an alternative to resin cartridges pre-mixed resinous mortar may be pumped into hole and tie-bar pushed in

Fig. 11.9   Resin-anchoring technique for installing facade-ties

columns and/or edges of its floor slabs. The most common method of allowing for differential movement here is to provide some form of slip surface between the new and existing elements which will prevent bonding of the two surfaces. The slip surface may comprise single or multiple layers of dense polythene or similar material, or a thin layer of fibre-board. Another accepted interface treatment is to leave a narrow gap where the new structure meets the facade to ensure that settlement may take place without damage. Typical interface treatments are shown in Fig. 11.13.

11.5 Foundation design

It is essential that the design and construction of the new structure does not adversely affect the stability of the retained facade, and this is of particular importance at foundation level. The foundations to many historic buildings are often found to be weak and unstable and are therefore vulnerable to any disturbance caused by new construction works. The two most common solutions used to overcome this problem are described here.

The first, and probably the simplest, method is to locate the outer column bases of the new structure some distance back from the retained facade and to cantilever the new floors from these columns to their junction with

the facade as shown in Fig. 11.14. This ensures that no new foundations are constructed adjacent to those of the facade, therefore ruling out any constructional disturbance and subsequent harmful effects caused by the new structure's loads.

The second method, illustrated in Fig. 11.15, is employed when the design of the new structure requires that some columns must be located immediately adjacent to the retained facade. In order to minimise disturbance at the base of the facade, the new column bases are constructed immediately adjacent to it, but do not undermine it. The new columns, which are also immediately adjacent to the facade, inevitably subject these bases to eccentric loading and an overturning effect, which must be counteracted in some way if the foundations are not to fail. The eccentric loads are 'balanced' by structurally connecting these bases to the axially loaded bases of an inner line of columns. This use of 'balanced-base' foundations counteracts the overturning effect which the columns adjacent to the facade have on their bases.

In certain facade retention schemes, some undermining and underpinning of the existing foundations is inevitable. In these cases it is of paramount importance that the new foundations are designed, and their construction phased, so as to minimise any adverse effects they may have on the stability of the retained facade.

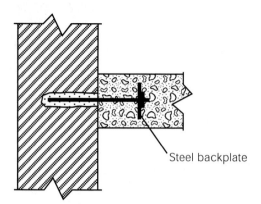

Projecting resin anchored tie bars cast directly into new concrete floor slabs with steel backplates to give lateral restraint

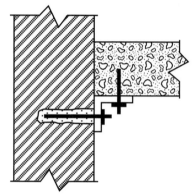

Underside of slab

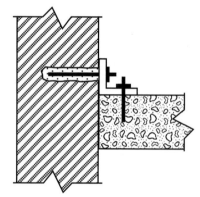

Upper surface of slab

Steel angles bolted to new floor slab and resin-anchored to facade masonry

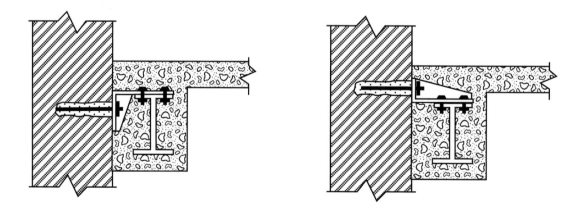

Purpose made steel angles bolted to beams of new steel frame and resin-anchored to facade masonry

Fig. 11.10 Various methods of connecting resin-anchors to the new structure

Fig. 11.11 Wholly internal temporary support system, St Paul's House, Park Square, Leeds. (Note resin-anchored facade-tie angle in bottom left corner)

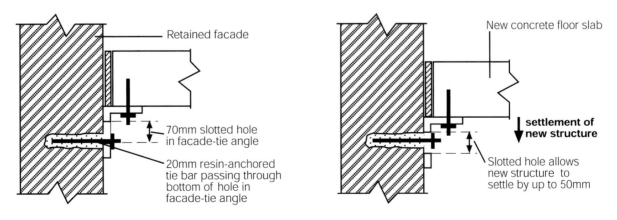

Fig. 11.12 Facade-tie design permitting settlement of new structure

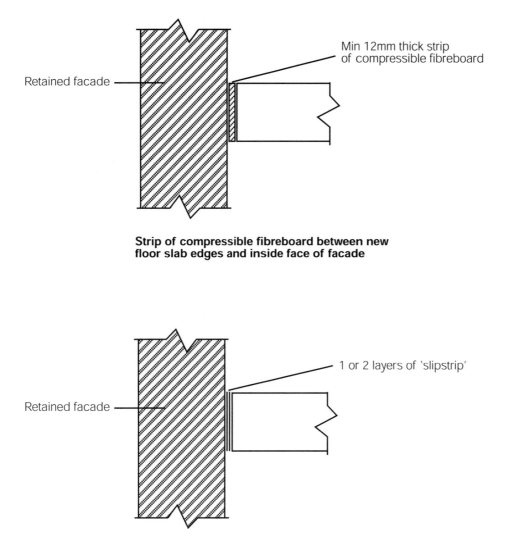

**Strip of compressible fibreboard between new
floor slab edges and inside face of facade**

**One or two layers of 'slipstrip' (e.g. dense polythene)
between new floor slab edges and inside face of facade**

Fig. 11.13 Interface details permitting settlement of new structure

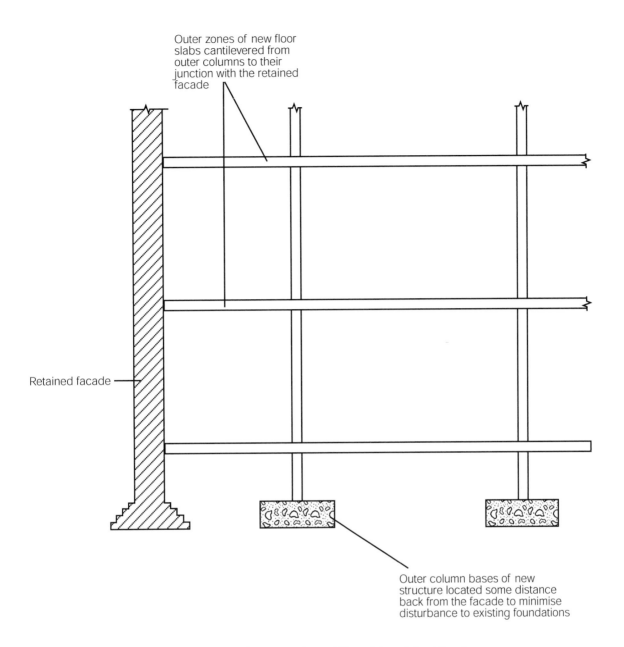

Outer zones of new floor slabs cantilevered from outer columns to their junction with the retained facade

Retained facade

Outer column bases of new structure located some distance back from the facade to minimise disturbance to existing foundations

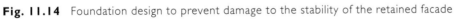

Fig. 11.14 Foundation design to prevent damage to the stability of the retained facade

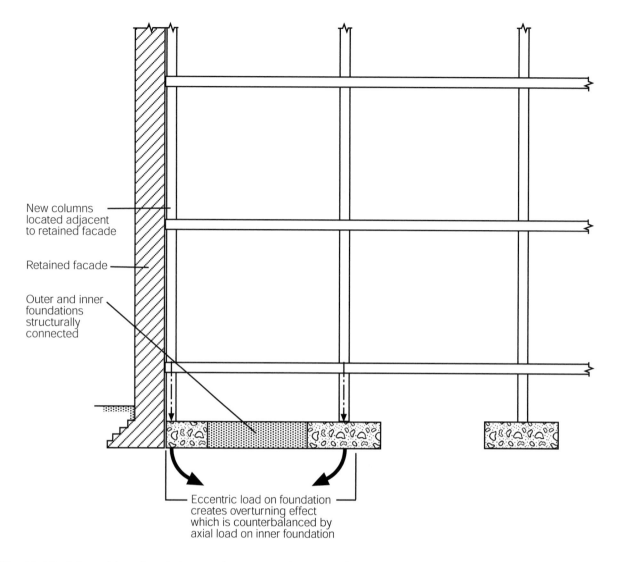

New columns located adjacent to retained facade

Retained facade

Outer and inner foundations structurally connected

Eccentric load on foundation creates overturning effect which is counterbalanced by axial load on inner foundation

Fig. 11.15 Balanced-base foundations used to prevent damage to the stability of the retained facade

References

Highfield, D. (1982) *The Construction of New Buildings behind Historic Facades: The Technical and Philosophical Implications*, M.Phil thesis, University of York.

Highfield, D. (1991) *The Construction of New Buildings behind Historic Facades*, E. & F.N. Spon, London.

Richards, J. (1994) *Facadism*, Routledge, London.

University of Bath, Department of Architecture and Building Engineering (1985) *Building Appraisal Maintenance and Preservation: Symposium Proceedings*, University of Bath.

12
Index of products and systems

Product/system	Referred to in Section	Manufacturer's/supplier's address	Contact no.
Supalux	2	Cape Calsil, Iver Lane, Uxbridge, Middlesex, UB8 2JQ	Tel. 01895 463000 Fax. 01895 259262
Masterboard	2		
Vermiculux	2		
Mandolite CP2	2	Mandoval, Douglas Drive, Catteshall Lane, Godalming, Surrey, GU7 1JX	Tel. 01483 425326 Fax. 01483 426881
Nullifire	2	Nullifire Ltd., Torrington Avenue, Coventry, CV4 9TJ	Tel. 01203 855000 Fax. 01203 469547 e-mail: protect@nullifire.com http://www.nullifire.com
Vicuclad	2	Promat Fire Protection Ltd., Meldreth, Royston, Hertfordshire, SG8 5RL	Tel. 01763 262310 Fax. 01763 262342 e-mail: promat@promat.demon.co.uk http://www.promat.co.uk
Sprayed Limpet Mineral Wool – GP Grade	2	Thermica Ltd., Stoneford House, Chamberlain Road, Stoneferry, Hull, HU8 8HH	Tel. 01482 329618 Fax. 01482 227723 e-mail: sales@thermica.co.uk http://www.thermica.co.uk
Tilcon Foamed Perlite	2	Tilcon (South) Ltd., Hornhouse Lane, Kirkby, Liverpool, L33 7YG	Tel. 0151 548 2676 Fax. 0151 548 4980
Thistle Renovating Plaster & Finish	3	British Gypsum Ltd., East Leake, Loughborough, Leicestershire, LE12 6JT	Tel. 0115 945 1000 or 0990 456123 Fax. 0990 456356 e-mail: technical.enquiries@bpb.com http://www.british/gypsum.bpb.com
Thistle Dri-Coat	3		
Thistle Finishes	3		
Gyproc Wallboards	3		
Gyproc Dri-Wall MF System	3		
Dri-Wall Adhesive & Sealant	3		
Gyproc Thermal Laminates	3		
Gyproc Dri-Wall TL System	3		
Gyproc Dri-Wall RF System	3		
Gyproc Gypliner Wall Lining System	3		

continued . . .

Product/system	Referred to in Section	Manufacturer's/supplier's address	Contact no.
Evo-Stik Floor Level and Fill	3	Evode Ltd., Common Road, Stafford, ST16 3EH	Tel. 01785 257755 e-mail: evo-stik@evode.co.uk http://www.evode.co.uk
Thermalath	4	BRC Building Products, Carver Road, Stafford, ST16 3BP	Tel. 01785 222288 Fax. 01785 240029 e-mail: @brc-building-products.co.uk
Isowool Timber Frame Batts	4	British Gypsum Ltd., East Leake, Loughborough, Leicestershire, LE12 6JT	Tel. 0115 945 1000 or 0990 456123 Fax. 0990 456356 e-mail: technical.enquiries@bpb.com http://www.british/gypsum.bpb.com
Gyproc Thermal Board	4		
Gyproc Thermal Board Plus	4		
Gyproc Thermal Board Super	4		
Isowool General Purpose Roll	4		
Gyproc Wallboard Duplex	4		
Roofmate SL	4	Dow Construction Products, 2 Heathrow Boulevard, 284 Bath Road, West Drayton, Middlesex, UB7 0DQ	Tel. 0181 917 5050 Fax. 0181 917 5413
Roofmate LG	4		
Styroliner LK	4	Panel Systems Ltd., Units 3–9, Welland Close, Rutland Road, Sheffield, S3 9QY	Tel. 0114 275 2881 Fax. 0114 276 8807 or 0114 278 6840
Styrofloor	4		
Rockwool RockShield rigid slabs	4	Rockwool Ltd., Pencoed, Bridgend, CF35 6NY	Tel. 01656 862621 Fax. 01656 862302 http://www.rockwool.co.uk
Rockwool EnergySaver cavity wall insulation	4		
Rockwool Rollbatts	4		
Rockwool EnergySaver blown loft insulation	4		
Rockwool Hardrock	4		
Expolath Polystyrene	4	Weber & Broutin UK Ltd., Dickens House, Maulden Road, Flitwick, Bedford, MK45 5BY	Tel. 01525 718877 Fax. 01525 718988
Terratherm PSB	4		
Terratherm PSM	4		
Gyproc SoundBloc Wallboard	5	British Gypsum Ltd., East Leake, Loughborough, Leicestershire, LE12 6JT	Tel. 0115 945 1000 or 0990 456123 Fax. 0990 456356 e-mail: technical.enquiries@bpb.com http://www.british/gypsum.bpb.com
Isowool Batts	5		
Gyproc SI Floor	5		
Isowool General Purpose Mineral Wool Roll	5		
Gyproc Independent Wall Lining System	5		

Product/system	Referred to in Section	Manufacturer's/supplier's address	Contact no.
Akustofloor	5	Panel Systems Ltd., Units 3–9, Welland Close, Rutland Road, Sheffield, S3 9QY	Tel. 0114 275 2881 Fax. 0114 276 8807 or 0114 278 6840
Gyproc Thermal Board Gyproc Thermal Board Plus Gyproc Thermal Board Super Gyproc Duplex Wallboard	6 6 6 6	British Gypsum Ltd., East Leake, Loughborough, Leicestershire, LE12 6JT.	Tel. 0115 945 1000 or 0990 456123 Fax. 0990 456356 e-mail: technical.enquiries@bpb.com http://www.british/gypsum.bpb.com
Tough-Cote Superflex RW2	6	Glixtone Ltd., Westminster Works, Alvechurch Road, West Heath, Birmingham, B31 3PG	Tel. 0121 243 1122 Fax. 0121 243 1123 e-mail: glixtone@aol.com
Evode Cementone Water Seal	6	Evode Ltd., Common Road, Stafford, ST16 3EH	Tel. 01785 257755 e-mail: evo-stik@evode.co.uk http://www.evode.co.uk
Newlath 2000 Newton System 500	6 6	John Newton & Co. Ltd., 12 Verney Road, London, SE16 3DH	Tel. 0171 237 1217 Fax. 0171 252 2769 e-mail: newtons@newton-and-co.co.uk http://www.newton-and-co.co.uk
Liquid Plastics K501 Monolastex Smooth Monolastex Textured	6 6 6	Liquid Plastics Ltd., Astral House, PO Box 7, Miller Street, Preston, Lancashire, PR1 1EA	Tel. 01772 259781 Fax. 01772 882016 e-mail: info@liquidplastics.co.uk http://www.liquidplastics.co.uk
RIW Liquid Asphaltic Composition RIW Flexiseal	6 6	RIW Ltd., Arc House, Terrace Road South, Binfield, Bracknell, Berkshire, RG42 4PZ	Tel. 01344 861988 Fax. 01344 862010
Thoroseal	6	HSC UK Ltd., 19 Broad Ground Road, Lakeside, Redditch, Worcestershire, B98 8YP	Tel. 01527 505100 Fax. 01527 510299
Spry Seal System	6	Spry Products, 64 Nottingham Road, Long Eaton, Nottingham, NG10 2AU	Tel. 0115 973 2914
Glidevale Twist & Lock Soffit Ventilators Glidevale Spring Wing Soffit Ventilators Glidevale Universal Rafter Ventilators Glidevale Tile and Slate Ventilators	6 6 6 6	Willan Building Services Ltd., 2 Brooklands Road, Sale, Cheshire, M33 3SS	Tel. 0161 962 7113 Fax. 0161 905 2085 e-mail: info@willan.co.uk http://www.willan.co.uk

Product/system	Referred to in Section	Manufacturer's/supplier's address	Contact no.
Ultra Tough Wood Filler system	7	Cuprinol Ltd., Adderwell, Frome, Somerset, BA11 1NL	Tel. 01373 475000 Fax. 01373 475050
Wykamol timber injection system Wykamol Boron Gel 40 Wykamol PJG Boron Rods	7 7 7	Philip Johnstone Group Ltd., Tingewick Road, Buckingham, MK18 1AN	Tel. 01280 823823 Fax. 01280 813910
Timber beam strengthening system	8	RTT Restoration Ltd., Brooklands Approach, North Street, Romford, Essex, RM1 1DX	Tel. 01708 725127 or 01708 764576 Fax. 01708 746899
Heavy-lifting systems	9	Abbey Pynford plc., Special Contracts Div., Unit 7, Bridge Works, Woodhead Road, Honley, Huddersfield, HD7 2PW	Tel. 01484 660003 Fax. 01484 660007 e-mail: hudsales@abbeypynford.co.uk http://www.abbeypynford.co.uk
Underpinning systems	10	Roger Bullivant Ltd., Walton Road, Drakelow, Burton-on-Trent, Staffordshire, DE15 9UA	Tel. 01283 511115 Fax. 01283 512233
Facade support systems	11	RMD Ltd., Stubbers Green Road, Aldridge, Walsall, WS9 8BW	Tel. 01922 743743 Fax. 01922 743400 e-mail: info@uk.rmdformwork.com http://www.rmdformwork.com

Index